Making Hats

Making Hats

Peter Morgan

B T Batsford Limited   London

© Peter Morgan 1971
First published 1971
Reprinted 1978 — first paperback edition

ISBN 0 7134 1078 7

Filmset by Filmtype Services Limited, Scarborough, Yorkshire
Printed in Great Britain by J W Arrowsmith Limited, Bristol
for the publishers
B T Batsford Limited
4 Fitzhardinge Street, London W1H 0AH

Contents

Section One Basic tools and equipment

Basic tools and blocks

Kettle Figure 1 (a) An ordinary kettle will make sufficient steam. Do not overfill or let it boil dry. A steamer with 2 or 3 spouts is not necessary for the home hat maker.

Iron (b) This should not be too heavy. A small flat electric iron is better than a gas heated one.

Egg iron (c) This is used for the making of spartre foundation shapes, the shaping of felts and covering materials. The egg-shaped head, which is heated in a gas flame, is set on a wooden handled stem. It is held in a table clamp when both hands are needed for working.

Sewing machine (d) Although the bulk of the work in hat making is done by hand, a machine is used quite often for top stitching crowns and brims of covered hats. Most people will find a hand machine easier to use than an electric one for these sort of tasks.

Pliers (e) A good pair is essential. They are used for cutting and bending wire, and should be narrow ended and easy to handle.

Spiral (f) This expandable metal ring holds felt, leno, etc. on the block while it is being steamed and manipulated into shape. Beware of catching fingers!

Scissors (g) Two pairs, one for cutting spartre, leno and other foundation shapes, and a better pair for fabrics. This pair should have a cutting blade of about 102 mm (4 in.).

Stanley knife (h) Used for cutting felts on the block. A razor blade will do.

Whale bone (i) This helps when easing leno and net shapes off the block.

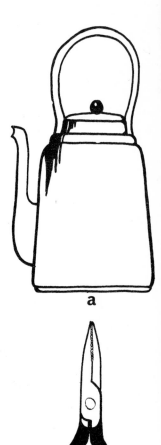

a

e

6

Figure 1 *Basic equipment*

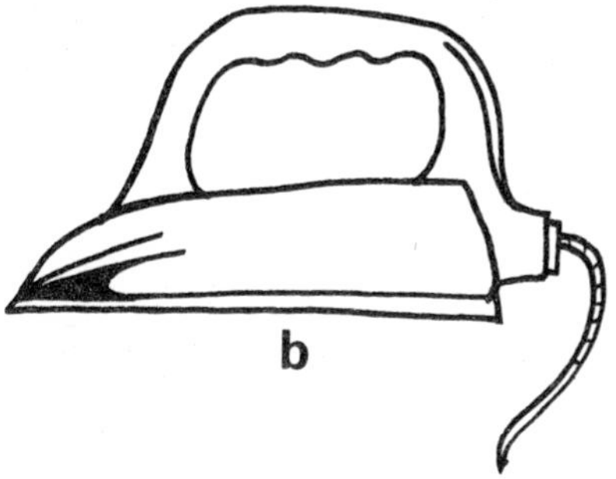

b

c

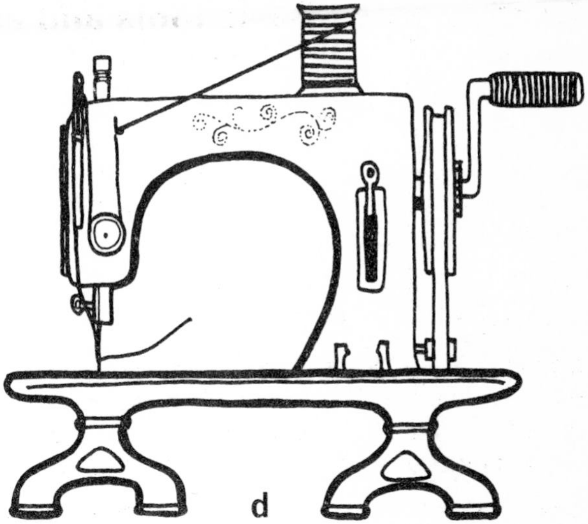

d

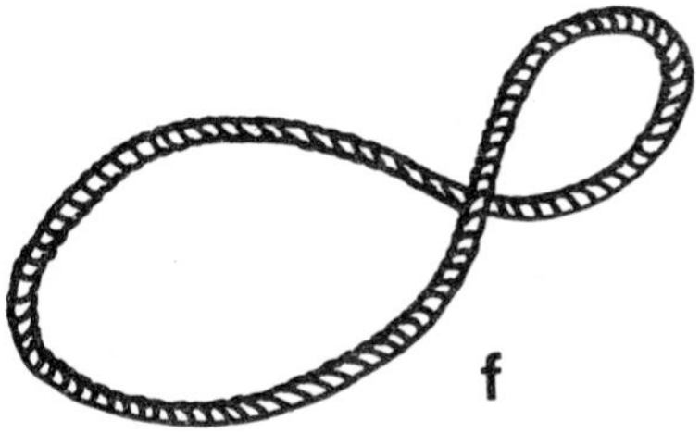

f

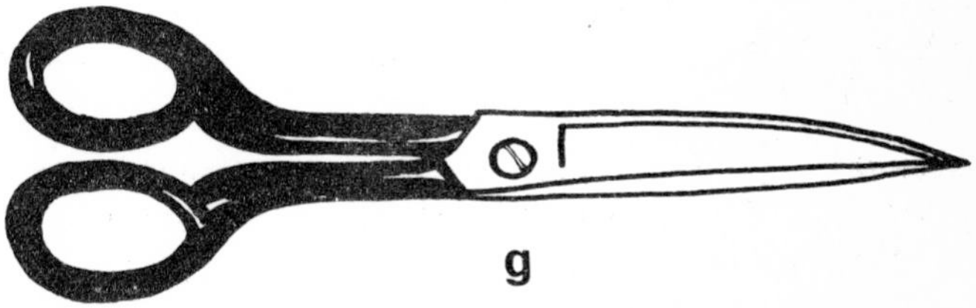

g

h

i

Tailors chalk   *Figure 2 (a)*   White and coloured for marking fabrics. Can be bought in pencil form.

Brushes (b)   One brush each, about 25 mm (1 in.) across for straw stiffener, felt stiffener and spartalac. Clean thoroughly after use.

Tape measure (c)   One of the non-stretch variety.

Pins (d)   Steel dressmaker pins 30 mm ($1\frac{3}{16}$ in.) for most work. *Lillikin* pins for velvet are useful. Be careful not to steam with pins in, otherwise marks may be left that will not come out.

Drawing pins (e)   These are used on most occasions when a hat is being blocked. They come under considerable strain, so ordinary domestic pins are too fragile. Use the heavier variety and do not leave the points in the block if the head comes off, as these will snag materials next time the block is used.

Needles (f)   Normal length needles are too short for millinery work, so longer needles, *straws* are used. The use of needles is basic common-sense. The finer the fabric, the finer the needle (suede and leather are exceptions—here a fine needle is better). Size 5 or 6 for heavy block spartre work, 7 or 8 for felts and foundation shapes, 9 or 10 for satins, chiffons and exceptionally fine work. A heavy curved needle *(g)* is a useful asset for block making.

Thimble (h)   Very necessary because of the pressure needed when pushing needles through heavy block work. A metal one is preferable to the plastic variety.

Pressing pads (i)   These are used when pressing is being done in the hand, which is quite frequently. I have found that a clean linen teatowel is quite sufficient and can be rolled or folded into the shape required.

Damping cloth   Normally a square (about 38 mm or 15 in.) of white fairly firm cotton which is used for damping or pressing fabrics into shape.

Pencil (j)

Figure 2 Basic equipment

a

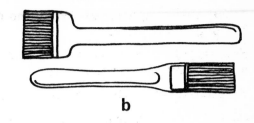
b

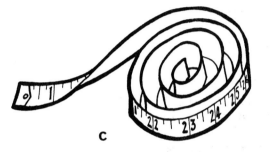
c

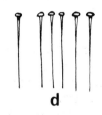
d

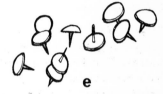
e

f

g

h

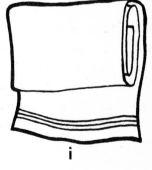
i

j

Figure 3 *Wooden blocks*

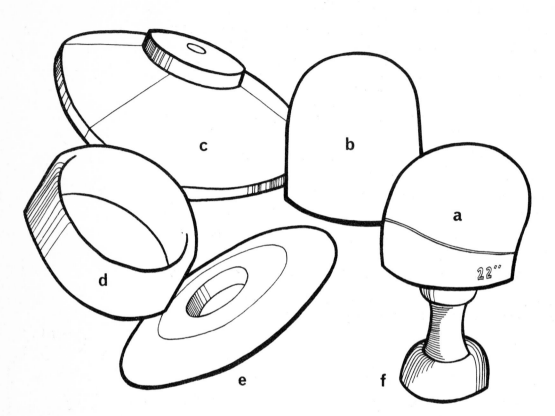

Wooden blocks   Wooden basic blocks are made from 500 to 588 mm (20 to $23\frac{1}{2}$ in.) head and graded in 13 mm (half inches).

Skull block   Figure 3 (a)   This has a shaped neck and is bought to the measurements of the wearer. Measure round the head from the top of the forehead to just under the 'bulge' at the back of the head for head size and from centre forehead over the head to centre back for crown depth. These measurements can be marked on the block for your correct fitting.

Dome crown block (b)   This is oval and symmetrical in shape and is one of the more useful basic shapes.

Beret block   Can be full, high domed and rounded, or comparatively flat. There are many varieties.

Brim blocks (c)   Again a great variety of shapes, small and large. The smaller head size is more useful because larger sizes can be taken from it.

Ring blocks (d)   Oval or round for steaming and stretching materials for trimmings and brims.

Shaped blocks   A variety of shapes according to fashion and popularity.

Ribbon discs (e)   A round flat disc used for the shaping of edge ribbons and materials which are steamed over the wedge shaped edge.

Block stand (f)   for supporting the various blocks while in use.

Linen head   Figure 4   is useful as a working stand and for finishing off with trimmings. The wooden heads are heavy and unnecessary.

   For anyone other than the professional milliner, only the skull block and stand are essential. The others can be obtained when experience will justify their purchase and put them to their full use.

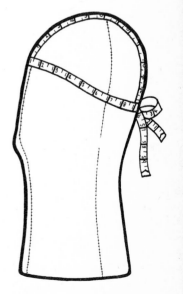

Figure 4   *Linen head showing correct position for taking head measurements*

Basic foundation materials

Esparterie Usually referred to as spartre, this is one of the most widely used of all foundation shapes. It comes in a variety of fine and heavy versions. It is a coarse open weave straw with a layer of muslin on one side. When dampened or steamed it will make practically any shape required and retain the shape when it is dry. It is used for making basic blocks and is covered in fabric when making hats.

Dior net A brittle very open net made in many colours and two sizes. It is used for transparent hats and as a foundation for very open flower or petal hats. Softens up when steamed into shape.

Leno is a loosely woven muslin usually used double for shapes. It has a 'filling' which becomes tacky when being steamed, but when dry holds the blocked shape well. It can also be used for binding edges and wire.

Foam This can be used in a similar manner to leno where the foam and outside fabric are machined and worked as one.

Tarlatan Slightly finer than leno. They both make good interlining for softer unblocked hats.

Stiffened lawn is also used for unblocked dressmaker hats but it can also be blocked.

Domette A stretchy woollen fabric, used as an interlining under fine materials to stop any slight discrepancies of the foundation block showing. This is known as *mulling*.

Wire Figure 5 (f) Only four types need concern us. No. 24 (lace wire) used for fine light work, no. 6 for general purposes and no. 90 for making spartre blocks. Ribbon wire *(e)* is stranded wire woven into tape and is used mainly for bows and trimmings. All these wires come in white or black.

Piping wire *(h)* is a soft but thick wire that is covered by other materials as one would cover a piping cord.

Straw stiffener (c) This is a clear thin varnish used to strengthen straws. It is brushed over the inside of the hat when it has dried after the final steaming and is used on the outside to give a high gloss.

Felt stiffener (b) *Feltene* is a special stiffening varnish made for felts. Use sparingly on the inside of the hat when dry.

Spartalac (a) This is a thick white liquid brushed evenly on spartre blocks when block making. It forms a hard coating.

Spartalac thinners (i) For diluting spartalac when it is getting thick and unmanageable.

Keep all varnishes away from heat and make sure that the lids are firmly on, otherwise they will evaporate or discolour.

Millinery solution (d) A rubber solution used for sticking and covering materials to difficult foundation shapes.

Sewing threads (g) Black and white cotton is needed for basic work. Heavy 24/36 for spartre block making, medium 40 for wire and foundation shapes and coloured thread of varying thickness for covering materials, stitching and trimmings.

Figure 5 *Basic working materials*

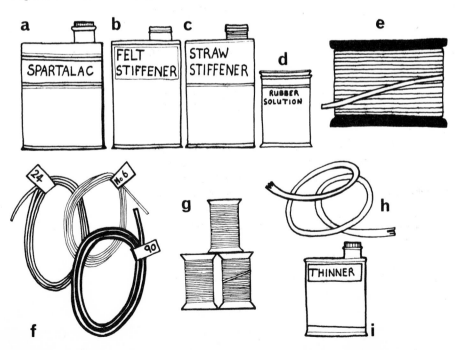

Section Two Stitches, wiring, linings, head finishes

Stitching

It is most important to use the right stitch for the right job. Most millinery stitches tend to be the same or a variation of those used in home dressmaking although there are a few used specifically for felt.

Darning The darning stitch is for making an invisible join when both sides of the work show simultaneously.

Oversewing The oversewing stitch is for oversewing a join on the wrong side of the fabric when the right sides are together.

Grafting The grafting stitch is similar to the oversewing stitch except that the felt is put edge to edge instead of right side to right side.

These three stitches are dealt with more fully in Section Four.

Stab stitch Figure 6 (a) This is a commonly used stitch made by 'stabbing' the needle neatly and evenly through from the inside to the outside of the hat and vice versa. The long side of the stitch is kept to the inside and the short stitch on the outside is kept as unobtrusive as possible. It can be used for headbands, inside and out, attaching trimmings, joining brims to crowns, holding folds in place, block making and many other uses.

   The length of the stitch will depend on the job it is doing. If there are too many stitches showing on the inside of the hat, it is best to insert a lining.

Upright hemming or whipping stitch (b) This stitch is used mainly for hemming down the turned over edge of a felt brim or 'invisibly' joining a felt crown and brim. The stitches should be neat and unobtrusive. A small vertical (upright) stitch is made to hold down the hem edge to the fabric and the needle is passed diagonally through the felt of the brim to re-appear in the hem about 6 mm ($\frac{1}{4}$ in.) to 10 mm ($\frac{3}{8}$ in.) away. Another small vertical stitch is made and the process repeated. This will make a very firm hem but do not let any stitches show on the right side of the brim. On the inside keep the stitches vertical and evenly spaced.

Slip stitch (c) The same stitch as for dressmaking. In millinery it is used a lot for finishing covered brim edges and inserting linings. Where the

Figure 6   (a) *Stab stitch*   (b) *Upright hemming or whipping stitch*   (c) *Slip stitch*

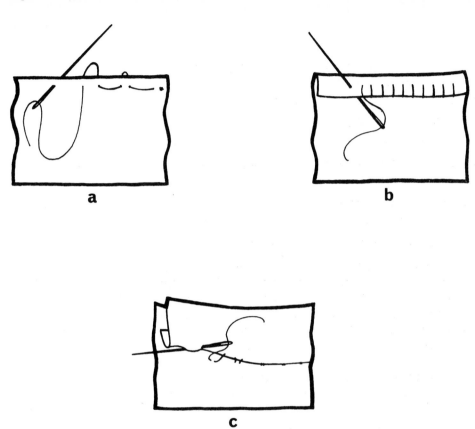

a

b

c

brim coverings are turned in and meet at the very edge, the stitch is slipped evenly into both folds going into the fold opposite from where it comes out of the other. The stitch is about 10 mm ($\frac{3}{8}$ in.) long.

Where the stitch is used for finishing a covered brim edge 'inside' the actual edge of the brim, or for attaching a sideband to a tip or inserting a lining, a longer stitch is made in the folded edge and a small stitch made in the fabric to which the edge is being attached. Make sure that this catching stitch does not show by placing it as much underneath the folded edge as is possible.

Figure 6   *(d) Diagonal stitch   (e) Back stitch*

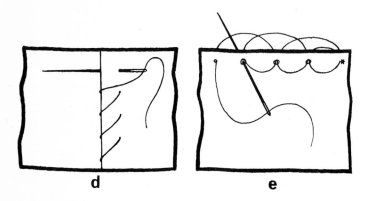

d   **e**

Diagonal stitch (d)   Although this stitch is normally used for holding two large areas of fabric together to prevent slipping, I have found it most useful when joining spartre tips and sidebands together. The shorter stitches are made parallel to each other on the wrong side so that the larger, slanting stitch appears on the right side.

Back stitch (e)   This stitch can be used for joining spartre together but other than that I have not found it to be very useful. Normally where you need to do a row of strong stitching, a machine, if it can be used, will make a firmer finish. To start this stitch, firmly attach the thread then make a fairly small stitch under the fabric, bringing the thread through and taking it back to the beginning of the stitch. Push through and then bring it out in front of the stitch you have just made. Take it back to the end of that stitch, and repeat the process. A larger version of the back stitch is very useful for joining fabric tip and sidebands or sectional crowns on the wrong side before they are machined as it will stop them slipping.

Figure 7   *(a) Taking the 'spring' out of wire*

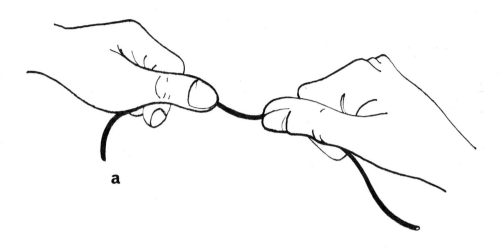

a

Wiring

It is essential to select the correct wire for the task that it has to perform. For extra fine delicate work use a lace wire. For normal work the slightly thicker no. 6 is most frequently used. Heavier wire is for making spartre blocks that need a very strong support. Do not overwire any hat as this will make it heavy to wear.

As the wire comes in a fairly tightly bound roll it must first be straightened otherwise the excess 'spring' in the wire will make it quite unmanageable. Pull the wire under the thumb, which presses against the forefinger, making sure that you are pulling against the curve. *Figure 7 (a).*

When wiring a net or transparent hat, the wire can be tinted with waterproof inks to match the foundation.

Figure 7   *(b) Wire stitch   (c) Joining wire together*

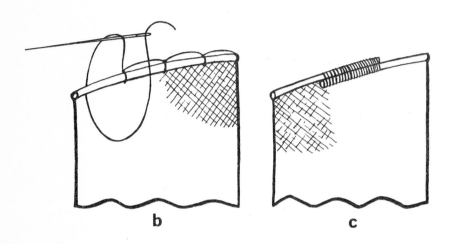

b   c

Wire stitch (b)   This extremely important stitch should be thoroughly mastered. It is for holding the wire on brim edges and headbands. It is made like a dressmaking buttonhole stitch with the stitches 13 mm ($\frac{1}{2}$ in.) to 19 mm ($\frac{3}{4}$ in.) apart. To start, oversew the wire two or three times to the edge of the brim foundation shape. Make a stitch about 13 mm ($\frac{1}{2}$ in.) to 19 mm ($\frac{3}{4}$ in.) along from the beginning but behind the wire and push the needle through the brim just underneath the wire. Do not pull tightly but leave a loop. Put the needle through the *back* of the loop, pull tightly and repeat. If you put the needle through the front of the loop rather than the back, it can slip and will not hold the wire very firmly. The knot should lie easily on the extreme outside edge of the wire.

Wiring brim edges (c)   Wire is nearly always used to give support and shape to the brim edge of hats. Measure off the required length of wire plus two or three inches which is used for an overlap at the back of the brim. When wiring spartre the wire is placed on the extreme edge of the spartre and stitched firmly in position with a wire stitch before the shape is covered. Start wiring from the centre back, stitching the two overlapping wires firmly together when finishing off.

Figure 7 *(d) Wiring in a fold*

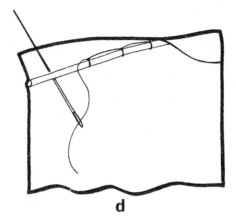

d

Wiring in a fold (d)   If a straw or felt is being wired, stitch the wire into the fold of the hem before the hem is finally turned and stitched, taking care that the stitching does not show on the brim edge. If you use this method, measure the length of wire, including the overlap, very accurately, and join the wire to form a circle. To do this, bind the overlapping wires tightly together so that they will not slip. It is possible, with this method, to machine the wire in position using a zip-foot pressed close up to the wire. However, tack the wire securely into position beforehand.

When any wire has to make a sharp turn rather than a gradual curve, it is advisable to bend it deftly with pliers. Never try to break wire by twisting it because you will not get a clean cut edge and the covering will unravel. Use the cutting edge of the pliers.

Linings

It is not always necessary to line a hat but if the inside is rather untidy a lining will give a much neater finish. Linings can be in toning or contrasting colours—a plain coloured hat could have a patterned lining. There are no rules about what can or what cannot be done, although it is advisable to keep linings light in weight. Taffeta, jap silk or any reasonably lightweight dress lining material is perfectly adequate.

Tip and sideband lining   Figure 8 (a)   This type can sometimes be bought in large stores but the colour range is generally restricted to black and white. As this lining is so easy to make, it is much more satisfying to make one's own.

Cut out the tip by using the bottom of a dome or similar block as a pattern. This includes 19 mm ($\frac{3}{4}$ in.) turnings all round. Cut the sideband on the cross grain of the fabric. Its length will have to measure the circumference of the crown plus 38 mm ($1\frac{1}{2}$ in.) which will give a 19 mm ($\frac{3}{4}$ in.) back seam. The width will be the depth of the crown plus a 19 mm ($\frac{3}{4}$ in.) turning. I do not think that it matters whether the back seam is stitched together vertically or diagonally.

Mark the tip in eighths by folding and do the same to the sideband. Pin the folded points together getting rid of the excess material in the sideband by forming pleats which must all lie in the same direction. As the tip will be oval, rather than round, line up its centre back carefully with the seam of the sideband. The centre back point on a sideband with a diagonal seam will be the centre of the seam itself. Machine the tip and sideband together with a 19 mm ($\frac{3}{4}$ in.) seam. Trim both seams down to about 10 mm ($\frac{3}{8}$ in.) and press. Turn the raw edge under about 13 mm ($\frac{1}{2}$ in.), insert into the hat and slipstitch into position. If the hat is to have a petersham headband the lining is stuck or tacked into the crown before the headband is attached. Remember to put the centre back of the lining to the centre back of the hat.

Sectional lining (b)   When making a sectional crown from a flat pattern, use the same pattern to make the lining. Insert into the hat by one of the methods given previously.

Figure 8 *(a) Tip and sideband lining* *(b) Sectional lining*

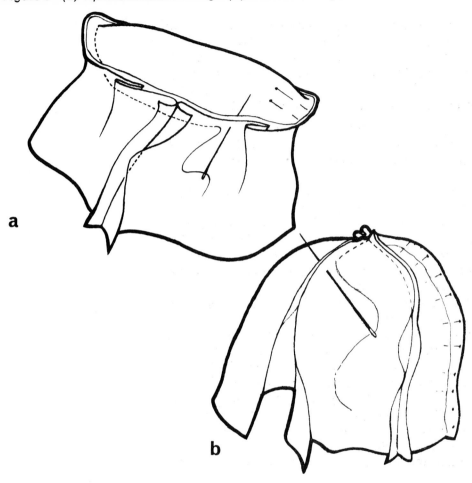

a

b

Net linings If a hat is partially see-through, eg, a dior net base with scattered flowers, an opaque lining will spoil the effect and look completely wrong. On these occasions, a lining of tulle or net that has been blocked on the same block as the hat of which it is a lining, is best. It can then be stuck or stitched on the crown and a headband inserted.

Figure 8 *(c) Curving a petersham ribbon on a linen head for a headband*

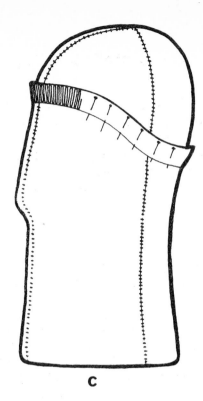

c

Headbands

No. 3, 13 mm or ($\frac{1}{2}$ in.) petersham ribbon is quite sufficient for headbands. Dampen and slightly curve the ribbon by stretching one edge while ironing with a warm iron. Cut off the required length, the head measurement plus 25 mm (1 in.) for turnings, by measuring the smaller unstretched edge. Turn one end in 13 mm ($\frac{1}{2}$ in.) and slipstitch the unstretched edge to the crown, starting at the centre back. When you have finished stitching the band, there should be 13 mm ($\frac{1}{2}$ in.) left over which is turned in and slipstitched to the other end of the ribbon. Steam lightly and press carefully. Although I have always found this method quite sufficient some people might prefer to completely pre-shape the ribbon to the head fitting of the block that is being used. This is done by pinning and steaming the ribbon into the required shape.

If the hat is a little larger than the head fitting then it must be eased *evenly* on to the headband all the way round. To do this, accurately mark the centre front, centre back and centre sides (midway between centre front and centre back) of the crown and the headband, and pin these points together before stitching.

Section Three Constructing and covering shapes

Making and covering a blocked shape is the method by which flat materials can be formed into three-dimensional shapes. It is not at all difficult once a few basic processes have been learned. There are various materials which are used for the foundation shapes and because it is possible to use practically any clothing fabric, as well as special millinery materials, the choice of covering materials is almost limitless.

Foundation materials

Spartre is the most widely used foundation material. It is a coarse open weave straw with a layer of muslin on one side and comes in fine and heavier weights. It is steamed and manipulated into shape either in the hand or over a block. It can also be dampened with a sponge on the straw side to pre-soften it if it is very brittle. Do not overwet it or the muslin will slide and peel off the base. The straw side is the wrong side and this always goes to the inside of the hat leaving the smoother muslin side next to the covering fabric. The straw, being very resistant, can easily snap, so if it is necessary to fold it, always have the straw side on the inside to prevent cracking.

Dior net is a brittle very open millinery net available in a variety of colours and sizes. This is also steamed and pulled over blocks to form foundation shapes but it is not as strong as spartre and for this reason it is sometimes used double. Be careful not to over-steam because it will go very limp and tear easily. It is the best foundation material for making very open, light summery hats.

Leno is a loosely woven muslin and because it is quite fine must be used double for blocking. It has a stiffening agent which becomes tacky when the leno is being steamed and blocked but this goes hard and holds the shape when it is dry. Leno is also cut into narrow bias strips which can be put over the edge of a wire brim or crown, etc. to finish it off with a smoother edge. It can also be ironed over spartre seams to give a better finish.

Foam This is available in several thicknesses and is used as a base for mounting the outside fabric. It gives a slight 'spring' in the seams and is excellent for sporty type hats. Care should be taken when machining because the foam can pull through the machine holes. It forms an excellent base for flat pattern hats and is one of the newer fabrics used in millinery.

Tarlatan is similar to leno but it does not block so well. Its main use is as a mounting fabric for flat pattern hats that need no blocking.

Covering materials

Velvet Of all the various covering materials, I have found velvet to be the most difficult and I would not recommend it to beginners. Because it marks so easily it must be handled as little as possible. If you have to put pins in, place them where any marks that might occur will not show, or use very fine needles. Velvet has a pile, so make sure you have it going in the direction you need before cutting into the fabric. The most successful way of pressing velvet is on a velvet board. This is a canvas-covered rubber board with hundreds of short pins standing up—rather like a bed of nails. The pile of the velvet falls between the pins and does not get pressed flat. It is possible to use a piece of velvet in place of a velvet board but this is not always satisfactory. Care should be taken when pressing seams open, press lightly and use a slightly damp cloth. A short piled millinery velvet is better than a dressmaking velvet.

Panne is a short or long haired velvet and is one of the most difficult of millinery materials because it marks so easily—definitely not for beginners. To 'turn' the pile, brush and lightly press with a warm iron alternately into the direction required.

Fur Dampen the pelt side and pin out taut on to a smooth surface to dry naturally. Lay the pattern pieces on to the skin making sure that the fur runs in the same direction, and cut cleanly with a razor blade. Place the edges together, there should be no turnings, and sew with a grafting stitch. Short haired furs are easier to work than long haired furs.

Leather is easy to work as long as it is not too thick and you have an accurate pattern. Use a fine needle to machine the pieces together, as this will penetrate the leather fibres more easily, and use a large stitch otherwise the leather can perforate and tear under tension. The seams can be stuck with rubber solution or top stitched down.

Lace This can be appliquéd on to a net foundation although it is possible to block lace by starching it first. For darker tones use felt stiffener because starch can cause discoloration.

Laize or strawcloth A piece-straw, usually synthetic, that comes in many weights, colours, textures and patterns. It is bought by the yard in a variety of widths and it is used as a woven fabric and can be varnished.

Satin Take care not to show pin marks. There should be no difficulty with other fabrics, such as chiffons, organdie, organza, fine wool, linen, cotton, silk, jersey, etc. Just remember to cut them on the cross so that they will drape and mould easily over the foundation shapes.

PVC coated fabrics make excellent rainproof hats but because the PVC coating does not allow the base fabric to stretch and give normally it is necessary to have an extremely accurate pattern. It is difficult to machine because it tends to stick under the machine foot. To combat this, machine it between pieces of fine tissue paper which can be torn away afterwards, or use talcum powder sprinkled liberally. Use a large stitch because a smaller one will cause the PVC to perforate and tear.

Plastics/acetate Sheets of coloured or transparent plastic or acetate of different gauges are sometimes used for more adventurous hats. It is best used as visors or inserts as it cannot be machined or stuck together successfully. If holes are punched through accurately it can be laced together most effectively.

Bias   Figure 9 (a)

Throughout this book materials are referred to as being cut on the bias or the cross. This might need an explanation. If you look at a handkerchief you will see that threads run over and under one another at a 90° angle. These are the warp and the weft. If you pull the handkerchief from corner to corner, you will find that there is hardly any stretch apart from any natural elasticity in the fibres themselves. This is the straight grain of a fabric. However, if the handkerchief is pulled diagonally from corner to corner there is a tremendous amount of stretch and play in the fabric. This is the bias or cross grain.

It is this attribute of any woven fabric that is taken advantage of in millinery. It is this that helps materials to ease and steam away when they are being blocked and makes soft folds rather than hard ones. When you make a seam in a bias cut piece of fabric, it can be made diagonally, following the straight grain, or made straight cutting across the bias of the fabric. In the latter case care has to be taken to make sure that the seam does not pucker or wrinkle.

Skinned join   (b) and *(c)*

This is the process by which spartre is joined to itself. At any seam make sure that there is about a 38 mm (1½ in.) overlap. Pin the seam together and peel back the muslin of the top piece of spartre about 51 mm (2 in.) Cut 19 mm (¾ in.) off this piece of spartre. Stitch the two pieces of spartre firmly together with a diagonal or back stitch *(b)*. Replace the muslin, dampen slightly and press with a warm iron until it has dried and stuck itself down *(c)*.

Headbands (d)   can be used to support brims or crowns while a shape is in the making. The shapes go on the inside of a headband and for this reason it is made 13 mm (½ in.) longer than the required head measurement. Cut a piece of spartre on the bias about 38mm (1½ in.) wide. The length will be the head measurement plus 38 mm (½ in.) allowance, plus turnings. Join the back seam together with a skinned join and wire both edges with a no. 6 wire. A headband can be pre-shaped to a block if necessary.

Figure 9   *(a) Bias   (b) and (c) Skinned join   (d) Headband   (e) Leno binding*

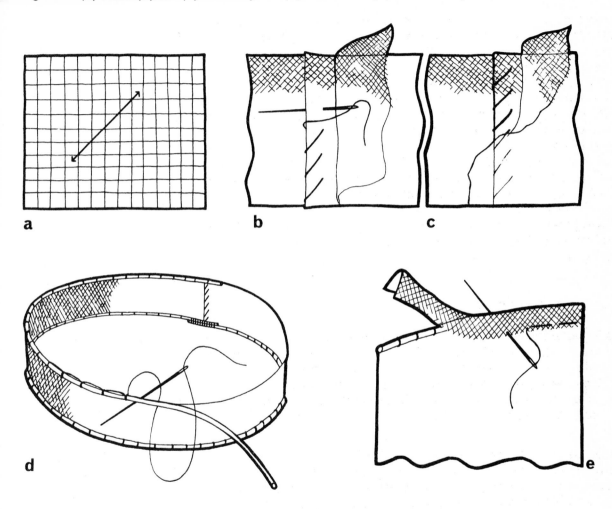

Leno binding (e)   This is a narrow strip of leno about 25 mm (1 in.) wide which is cut on the bias. It is folded along its length and stretched round the edges of wired brims and crowns to give a smoothly finished edge. It is held neatly in position with a stab stitch.

Blocking a spartre crown by the tip and sideband method *Figure 10.* Cut a piece of spartre 50 mm (2 in.) longer than the circumference of the block and 50 mm (2 in.) deeper than the depth of the required crown. This is to allow for shrinkage and trimming. Dampen the spartre so that it is pliable and line up the centre front of the spartre to the centre front of the block, placing the straw side to the inside. Pull the strip round the block so that the top part of the spartre starts to mould round the crown of the block. Keep the spartre constantly and evenly exposed to the steam, moulding and pulling out any excess with the fingers. Pull away from the straight grain into the bias. When you have got rid of all the excess spartre that is possible pin it down with drawing pins, steel pins on a spartre basic block. When it is dry, trim away the excess spartre at the top of the crown with a sharp pair of scissors. Join the back seam with a skinned join. A curved upholstery needle is sometimes easier than a straight one. I do not think that it matters whether the back seam is diagonal (following the straight grain of the spartre) or vertical (cutting across the bias). If it is a diagonal seam, have an equal amount of the seam either side of the centre back.

To make the tip cut a piece of spartre that will be large enough to cover the crown with about a 38 mm (1½ in.) overlap. Dampen with a sponge and place it on the crown, holding it in approximate position with three or four drawing pins, positioning the bias to the centre front. Steam and mould it over the crown pinning it to the sideband with steel pins so that it overlaps. This overlap will be trimmed down to about 25 mm (1 in.) so that it can be attached to the sideband with a skinned joint. The whole of the blocked shape, particularly the joins, should be well polished with a hot iron while it is still on the block to give a smooth surface. Mark the centre front and centre back with tailors chalk or a thread that can be removed. Do not use a heavy pencil or biro because if the marks are permanent they might show through a pale coloured covering fabric. When the spartre is completely dry, trim the bottom edge to the shape required and remove it from the block. If necessary this edge can be wired and covered with a leno binding. This will give a clean, well-defined edge and also stop it from stretching. The shape can be given a light coating of straw stiffener if needed on the inside.

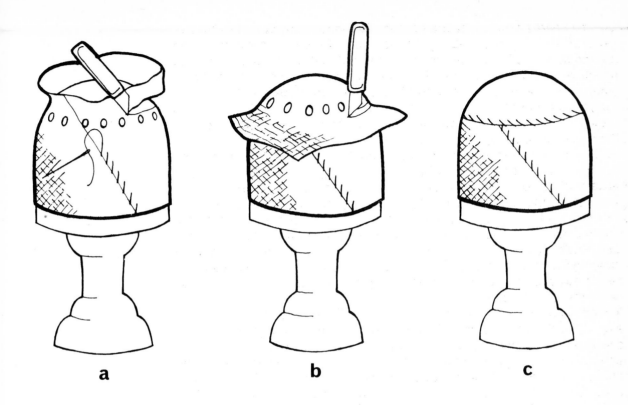

Figure 10   Blocking a spartre crown—tip and sideband method
(a) Sideband being trimmed after stitching   (b) Tip being attached
(c) Finished shape

Blocking a leno or dior net crown   Figure 11   In explaining this method I will just refer to leno although dior nets and tulle are also blocked in this manner.

A crown made from leno can be blocked in one piece. Cut a piece of leno about 457 mm (18 in.) square, or two pieces if working double. Steam the leno briefly until it starts to soften and place it over the block with the bias running from the centre front to the centre back. Ease a wire spiral over the block pulling it down to 25 mm (1 in.) below the required headline. Do this gently, otherwise the spiral can catch and tear the fabric. Shrink and stretch the folds out of the leno by pulling along and away from the straight grain into the bias. Steam constantly but do not get it too wet. After all the fulness has been eased out, but while it is still slightly damp, press hard with an iron using a circular motion. This will help the leno to really harden and set into shape. When the shape is completely dry, mark the centre front and centre back and remove it from the block. A whale-bone slipped inside and eased gently round is a considerable help as the leno can sometimes stick to the block. A fine sheet of polythene slipped under the net and blocked with it beforehand will make this job even easier. Wire, bind the edge with leno and stiffen on the inside with straw stiffener if necessary.

 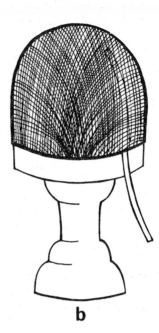

Figure 11   Blocking a leno or dior net crown
(a) Trimming away surplus material after crown has been steamed and blocked
(b) Easing crown off the block with a whale bone

Covering crowns

The choice of the covering material obviously influences the type of foundation that will be needed. Soft, lightweight materials will need leno or dior net bases—heavier, thicker ones will need firmer spartre bases. Having decided upon the most suitable foundation for your covering fabric you must now choose the most suitable method of actually covering the shape. This can depend on the type of fabric, its thickness, pliability, texture, pattern, quantity and of course, your design. There are not a lot of alternatives but it is worth finding and using the correct one.

All in one   This method can only be used where the crown is very shallow and the covering material is very stretchy, eg, jersey. Measure across the longest part of the crown, and using this as the diameter, cut a circle of fabric adding about 51 mm (2 in.) all round for turnings. Place the fabric over the shape easing the surplus into the bias. At the headline trim away any excess fabric leaving a 25 mm (1 in.) turning. Fold over into the inside of the crown and stitch down.

Tip and sideband—Method 1   Figure 12 (a) and (b)   For the sideband cut a rectangular piece, on the bias 38 mm (1½ in.) longer than the circumference of the crown and 51 mm (2 in.) deeper than its depth. Place the right side of the material to the block. Pull it round the foundation shape, which remains on the block, so that the top part clings to the curvature of the crown. Make a vertical seam at the centre back and trim down the turnings. Cut a piece of fabric for the tip, exactly as is done for a spartre tip, placing it on the block with the right side to the block. Pin the tip and sideband together and tack them firmly. This is to stop them slipping when the shape is removed from the block to be machined. It might be necessary to pin and re-pin the tip and sideband together two or three times before you have made a clean seam with no puckers and with the easing evenly distributed either side of the seam. After machining it is easier to put the shape back on to the block for trimming and pressing the seams. Turn the right side to the outside and slip it over the foundation shape, sometimes a brief steaming will help it to mould on to the shape. Trim the edge, leaving a 25 mm (1 in.) turning which is turned into the inside of the crown and stitched down.

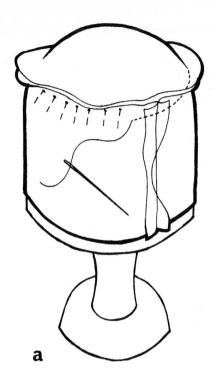 

Figure 12   Covering a crown—Tip and sideband, Method 1
(a) Tip is pinned to sideband and stitched   (b) Appearance of crown on the right
side

Tip and sideband—Method 2 Figure 12 (c) and (d) Cut out a tip and place it, right side up, on top of the crown. Pin it down so that the maximum amount of fabric can be eased away evenly all round. Stab stitch the tip down and cut away any excess turning. Cut and place the sideband on the block as in Method 1. The sideband must evenly overlap the tip by 13 to 19 mm ($\frac{1}{2}$ to $\frac{3}{4}$ in.). After the back seam has been stitched, remove the sideband from the block, turn it through and replace it with the right side outside again, making sure that the top edge evenly overlaps the tip. Turn the top of the sideband in and slip stitch it down to the tip. Press lightly, under a cloth, and finish as in Method 1.

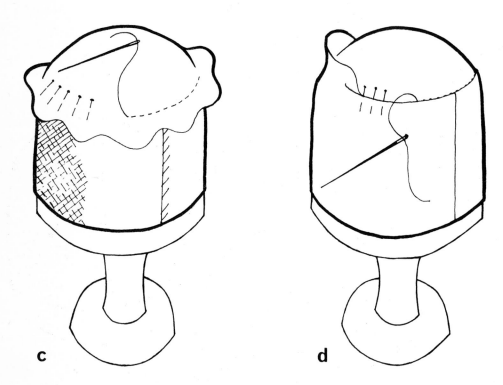

c   d

Figure 12 Method 2
(c) Tip stitched down to the top of the crown   (d) Sideband being turned in and slip stitched to the tip

Tip and sideband—Method 3, butted joins   Figure 13 (a), (b), (c) and (d)   A spartre crown is made in the normal manner and the tip is sliced off, rather like the top of a boiled egg. The covering fabric is carefully eased and turned over the edge of the tip so that it does not buckle. Stitch the turning down on the inside so that no stitches show on the outside and trim away any excess fabric leaving about 13 mm ($\frac{1}{2}$ in.) turning. Cover the sideband in the same manner. The tip and sideband are joined together by invisible slip stitches. This method is particularly suitable for velvet and thick fabrics because the turnings cannot print through to the outside.

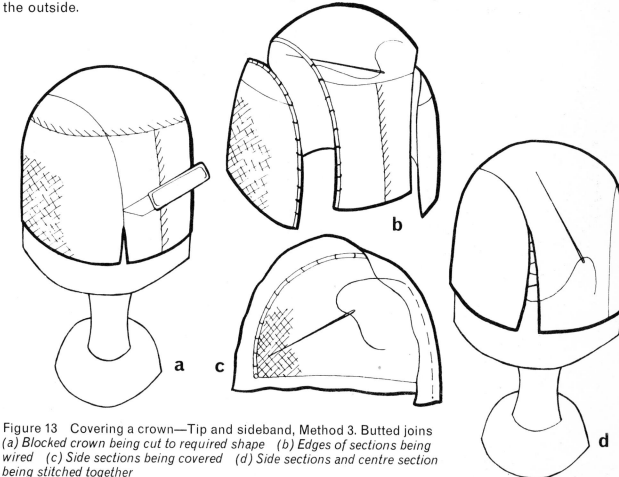

Figure 13   Covering a crown—Tip and sideband, Method 3. Butted joins
(a) Blocked crown being cut to required shape   (b) Edges of sections being wired   (c) Side sections being covered   (d) Side sections and centre section being stitched together

The crown can be cut in any sectional manner and if necessary the edge can be wired with a fine wire although this will add extra weight and should be avoided if possible.

Sectional crowns   Figure 14 (a) and (b)   The number and shape of the sections will depend upon the design which itself is influenced by the fabric. As a block is rarely uniform in shape all the way round, it is best to work on one half of the block and then to repeat these sections on the other half. The shape of the sections can be worked out approximately by taking measurements. The depth of a section will be from the base of the section to the tip. The width can be taken by measuring from seam to seam, using the depth measurement as a centre guide line, measuring along it every 25 mm (1 in.). If it is a four-sectioned crown, it will be a quarter of the circumference at the base and if it is a six-sectioned crown, one sixth, and so forth. Always cut the sections with the bias running from the tip to the base of the crown. Add turnings of about 25 mm (1 in.) all the way round each section, place them on the block, right side inside, and then pin together. When the sections are satisfactory, trim the seams down, remove from the block and use these sections as patterns for the other half of the hat. Put all the sections back on again to make sure that it is a good fit and then tack the panels of each half firmly together. Always stitch from the tip to the base of the crown. When the panels are stitched together one half of the hat is done first and then the other. The two halves are then accurately tacked together, making sure that all the panels meet at the centre of the tip, and machined in one long seam from one end to the other. Trim and press the seams flat, turn through and replace on the foundation shape, steaming it if necessary. Finish the base of the crown as in the previous methods.

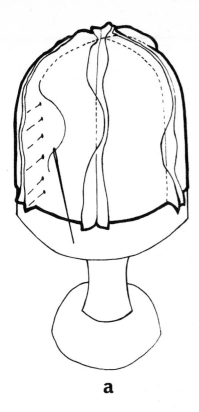 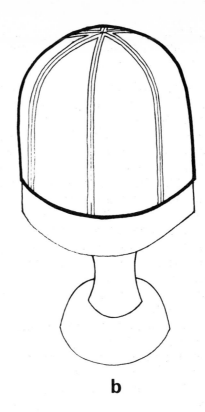

a   b

Figure 14   Sectional crown
*(a) Six-sectioned crown being stitched together   (b) Appearance of the crown
on the right side, the seams having been top stitched*

Three-sectioned crown   Figure 15 (a) and (b)   This has two half-moon shaped side panels and one centre panel that runs over the crown from the centre front to the centre back. It is not difficult to do but make sure that the side panels are identical. Before cutting the panels you must decide approximately where the seams are going to be as their shape will depend on this factor. Sometimes the position of the seam is dictated by the fact that the fabric will not ease away any more after a certain point. If the material is very stretchy this will probably not occur. As a rough guide on a dome block, the width of the centre panel would be about a quarter of the block circumference and the depth of a side panel would be about two thirds the measurement between the centre of the crown and a centre side point. As this is only an approximate guide, and as it will also depend upon material and design considerations, you must use your judgment. For the centre panel cut a rectangular piece on the bias. The length should be the measurement taken across the crown from the centre front to the centre back plus 51 mm (2 in.) and the width approximately a quarter of the circumference plus 51 mm (2 in.). Run a tacking thread along the centre of this panel and then place the fabric, right side down, over the block. Pin securely into position from the centre front to the centre back. Ease any fulness away from the centre line towards the side seam and pin down. You will then be able to judge the approximate shape needed for the side panels.

Cut these so that the bias runs from the top to the bottom of the crown. Pin one of the panels to the shape and ease any fulness towards the seam. Pin the side and centre panels together so that a visually satisfactory seam line is formed. Tack this seam together very firmly. To make sure that the two side panels are identical, measurements can be taken from the tacking line that indicates the middle of the centre panel out to the side seam. This is repeated exactly on the other side when the second panel is pinned into position. Machine the panels together, trim the seams, press, turn out the right way and finish as for the other methods.

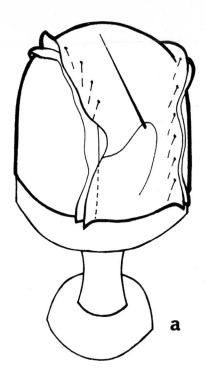 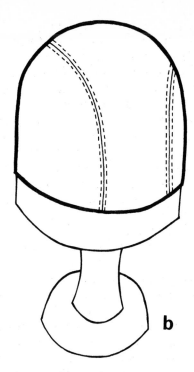

Figure 15 *(a) Three-sectioned crown being stitched together   (b) Finished crown on the right side*

Covering crowns with flowers, petals, etc   Figure 15 (c) and (d)   If the covering trimming is closely bunched together, there is no need to use an under-covering, but if the trimmings are rather sparse, cover first by one of the previous methods. For a hat with no brim the headline will probably need to be covered. Measure the circumference and cut a piece this length, on the bias, about 76 mm (3 in.) wide. Cover the bottom 51mm (2 in.) of the hat, as you would work a sideband, and fold the remaining 25mm (1 in.) inside, stitching both edges into place. When the hat is being covered with its trimmings they must be arranged to cover the raw edge of this band. When covering the foundation shape, usually leno or net with this type of hat, it is essential to start from the tip and work down to the base. If it is worked the other way the trimmings round the side can easily get crushed and tattered by the time that the final one has been placed on the tip. Attach the trimming at two or three points securely with a buttonhole stitch—a shorter length of thread is much easier to work with because it will not twist and get knotted. Keep the inside of the hat as neat as possible and do not leave loose threads hanging around. Insert a fine lining for neatness.

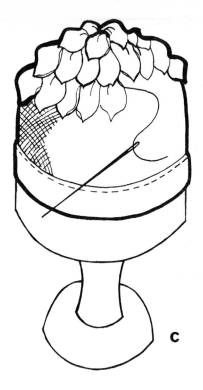 

Figure 15 *(c) Leno crown being covered with petals—crown edge has been covered with a crossway strip   (d) Finished petalled crown*

Figure 16   Draped crowns
(a) Crown is covered with folded crossway strips   (b) Finished regularly draped crown

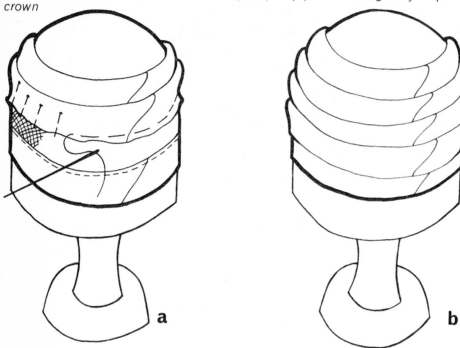

a

b

   Draped and folded crowns   Figure 16 (a), (b), (c) and (d)   This is one of the most difficult and challenging styles. One of the main faults of most beginners is that the folds are too tight and lifeless so that the overall effect is one of meanness. Practise on a block with various types of fabric and styles until you are satisfied that you can produce a worthwhile result. The only rule is to cut all your fabric on the bias and be generous with it. I will explain some of the ways in which a draped style can be produced, but there is no substitute for experiment nor are there any easy ways or short cuts.

   For an even, regular type of draping, cut strips of fabric on the bias, the circumference of the crown plus 51 mm (2 in.) for the length. The width is two to three times the width of the finished fold. Join each strip together with a diagonal seam and fold along the centre. This seam will be better than a vertical one because it will not give such a hard seamed effect at the back of the hat. Cut a crossway strip about 76 mm

(c) and (d) A more irregular way of draping a crown

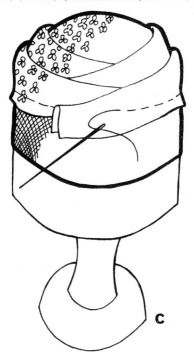

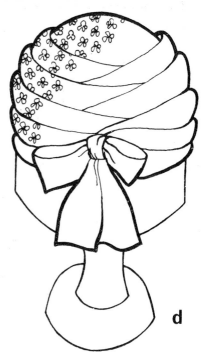

c

d

(3 in.) wide to cover bottom edge of the crown, as was explained in the previous method, and stitch on to the hat. Cover the crown with a tip, and stitch that into position. Pin the folds into place until you have an effect with which you are satisfied, arranging them so that each fold easily covers the edge of the previous one. Stab stitch the folds securely down so that they cannot slip, making sure that the line of a fold is not broken by a badly placed stitch. Finish the inside with a soft lining.

The other method is similar except that the effect is much more irregular. The lengths are cut longer so that they can be folded and interwoven with one another in a more varied manner. This can be done at the back, front, side of a hat, or wherever the design requires them to be. The folds can run right off the edge and be tucked inside the hat or a crossway binding and tip can be used as in the previous method.

With any draped style, be extravagant with the material, do not pull the folds too tightly, and do not overstitch. Above all, experiment.

Mulling Sometimes a covering material can be so fine, eg, chiffons and fine silks, that any slight discrepancy in the foundation shape becomes a glaring fault. To eliminate this, a fine interlining of domette is put between the covering material and the foundation shape. It is cut on the cross and placed on the shape by the tip and sideband Method 1. Do not seam it but put the domette edge to edge, stitching it firmly down but causing no ridges. Press slightly so that you have a smooth shape ready to be covered by the covering material. This process is mulling and can also be used for quilted effects.

General advice on covering

If a seam is to be top-stitched leave enough turning so that you can machine through a double layer of fabric. This will give slightly indented top stitching and looks more effective.

When covering any shape do not pull the fabric too tightly as this can cause the foundation shape to buckle.

Blocking a spartre brim

The method of blocking a brim will depend upon its size and shape. It can be made on wooden or spartre blocks, on a flat wooden surface or from a paper pattern.

Crossway brim   Figure 17 (a), (b) and (c)   This method can be used for a small, narrow brim. For the length measure round the brim edge and add 51 to 76 mm (2 to 3 in.). The width is the width of the block plus 51 to 76 mm (2 to 3 in.) which will allow for shrinkage. This strip is cut on the bias. Dampen the spartre and, starting at the centre front, pin the strip round the block, shrinking and easing away the fulness where necessary. Leave at least an extra 25 mm (1 in.) inside the headline for the turning that has to be attached to the crown. Trim away any extra fulness at the back and make a vertical or diagonal skinned join. When the spartre is dry, mark the exact position of the brim edge and the head fitting. Remove it from the block, trim, wire and bind the brim edge with leno. If necessary, a wire can be tacked up to the headline and the turning is snipped, about every 19 mm ($\frac{3}{4}$ in.) up to the wire. It is now ready to be covered.

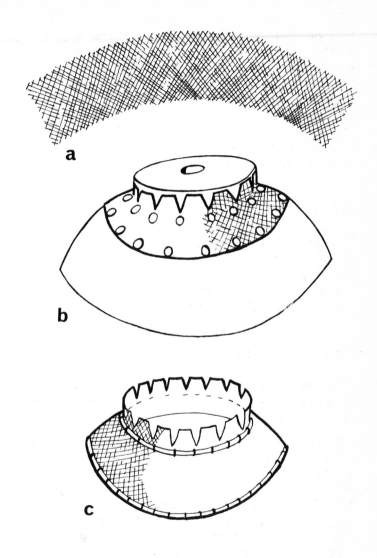

Figure 17   Blocking a spartre crossway brim
*(a) Length of bias-cut spartre   (b) Spartre pinned and steamed
round a suitable block   (c) Wiring of the brim edge and headline*

Large, shaped brims   Figure 18 (a), (b) and (c)   If the design has a large picture brim it is impossible to block it by the above method because of its size. Cut a piece of spartre 51 to 76 mm (2 to 3 in.) larger all round than the size of the brim block. Place the bias to the centre front, and, starting from that point, ease and shrink away as much fulness as possible. Stretch the spartre at the brim edge and shrink it at the headline. Do this evenly working towards the centre back. You will probably be left with a surplus of spartre at the back that will not shrink any more. Cut cleanly through this from the centre back brim edge to the centre of the piece of spartre. Cut away the surplus spartre at the crown, but leave a good 25 mm turning on the inside of the headline. Trim away the excess spartre along the cut at the back leaving enough to make a neat skinned join. Wire and bind the brim edge and headline as for the previous method.

Flat brim (d)   Place the bottom of the crown block on to a piece of spartre so that the centre front—centre back axis runs along the bias. Trace round with tailors chalk and fit a headwire about 3 mm ($\frac{1}{8}$ in.) just outside this line. Cut round 25 mm (1 in.) inside this line and snip down, about every 19 mm ($\frac{3}{4}$ in.) to the line. Cut a spartre band, on the bias, 38 mm (1$\frac{1}{2}$ in.) wide and the length of the headfitting plus turnings. Join the back seam and place this headband inside the headfitting and stab stitch it to the turnings. This gives the head fitting extra strength. Dampen the spartre and drawing pin it on to a flat board. When it is dry, measure the depth of the brim that is needed. The back is cut 19 mm ($\frac{3}{4}$ in.) narrower than the front to give the brim a balanced look on the head. Trim, wire and bind the edge and give the brim a coating of straw stiffener to help hold its shape.

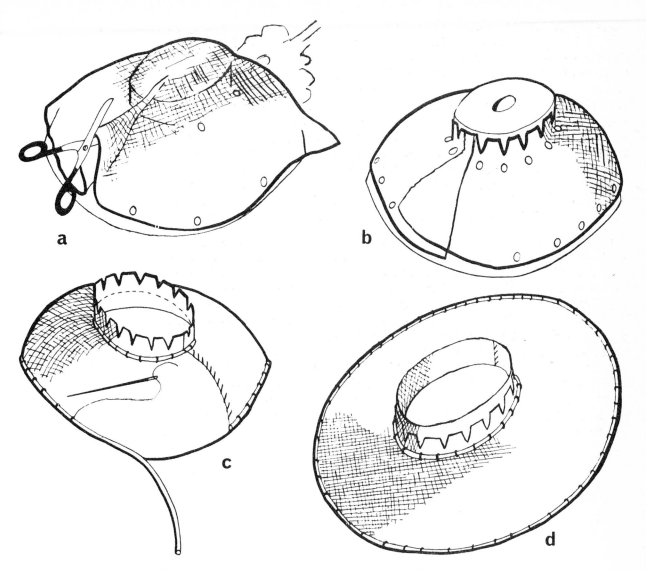

Figure 18 Large shaped brim *(a) Spartre being steamed and pinned over a suitable block (b) The brim is trimmed and cut to the correct shape (c) After the back seam has been joined, the brim is wired where necessary*
Flat brim *(d) It is wired and a crossway spartre headband fitted for strength and shape retention*

Figure 18
Leno brim   *(e) Preparing the leno or dior net crossway strip   (f) Finishing the brim by wiring and inserting a headband*

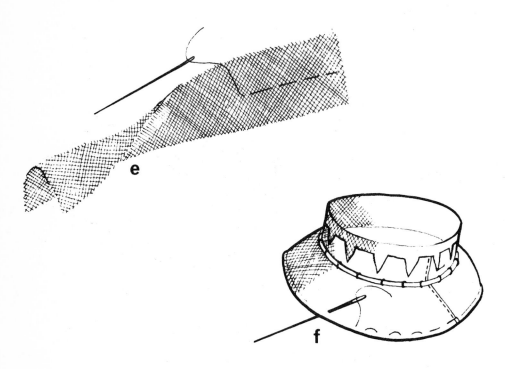

Leno and net brims   Leno and net are not really suitable for large brims but can be made in the same way as spartre brims if necessary, except that they are blocked double. See flat pattern brims, Section Six. Only the crossway brim is a little different.

Leno crossway brim   Figure 18 (e) and (f)   Cut the strip double the width that is needed for a spartre brim. Mark the centre along its length with tacking or tailors chalk. Keep this line on the brim edge when it is being steamed round the block. When it has dried, back stitch the leno together, both sides, to form a centre back seam, trimming away any surplus. Stitch a fine wire, lace or no. 6, into the fold and into the headline. Insert a headband if necessary and stiffen the shape with straw stiffener.

Figure 19   Manipulated brim
(a) Preliminary wiring and pinning of a crossway strip to a block for steaming and manipulating   (b) After a brim shape has been decided, the edge is trimmed and wired

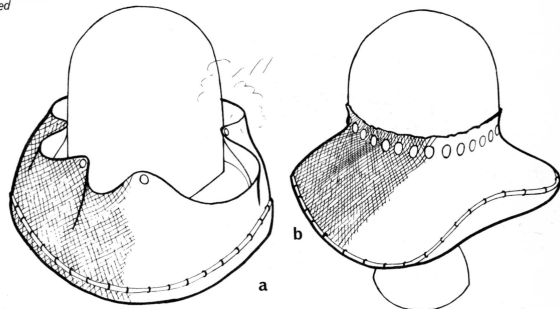

Manipulated brims   Figure 19 (a) and (b)   are worked in the hand by steaming and easing on to a headband or crown block. Cut a strip of crossway spartre about 51 mm (2 in.) longer and wider than the required brim circumference and width. Mark in the centre front, centre back and centre side positions and pin the brim edge on to a prepared wire. Now by stretching and shrinking in the steam manipulate the crown edge on to the headband and form the brim into the shape required. When it is dry, trim away the excess spartre and finish by skin joining the back seam and wiring the brim edge. The brim can be stiffened with straw stiffener.

If you have no brim block and wish to make a large sloping brim, you can use a pattern. Details of how to cut a flat pattern brim can be found in Section Six. Otherwise it is made in a similar way to the last method— back seam skin joined, head fitting wired, brim edge wired and leno bound.

When blocking all spartre brims, remember to keep the muslin side to the outside of the shape.

49

Covering brims

Crossway strip   Figure 20 (a) and (b)   This is used for covering fairly narrow brims. Cut a strip, on the bias, the length of the brim edge plus 51 mm (2 in.). The width will be double the width of the brim plus about 76 mm (3 in.) for turnings. Mark the centre of the strip along its length— this is a guideline which sits on the brim edge. Starting from the centre front, ease and stretch the strip over the foundation shape, holding it in place with pins. Be careful not to pull too tightly and buckle the brim. Get rid of the fulness into the headline and centre back seam. The back seam can be trimmed, turned in and slip stitched together, or the covering can be removed, machine stitched and then replaced. Back stitch the covering and foundation shape neatly together inside the headline.

Two part covering   (c), (d) and (e)   This method can be used for covering flat brims or large shaped ones. The underside of the brim is covered first. This is done by cutting a single crossway strip and using the above method or by covering the shape with a single piece of fabric. A single shape is normally used for flat brims. With a single piece, keep the bias to the front and pin down the brim edge and headline as the fulness is eased away. Take the surplus out of the back seam. When it fits accurately, mark the centre front and any other guide lines, and remove it from the foundation shape. Finish the back seam. Cover the underside of the block with rubber solution, do not get it too lumpy, and replace the underbrim, smoothing out any wrinkles. The top brim is completed in exactly the same way and then the brim edge can be completed.

Before using the rubber solution, try it out on a spare piece of the fabric to make sure that it will stick and that it does not seep through.

Figure 20   Covering brims—crossway strip   (a) *Preparing a crossway strip of fabric*   (b) *Fabric being eased over the brim*
Two-part covering   (c) *Attaching the underbrim covering to the spartre brim shape*   (d) *Attaching the top brim*   (e) *Finishing the brim covering*

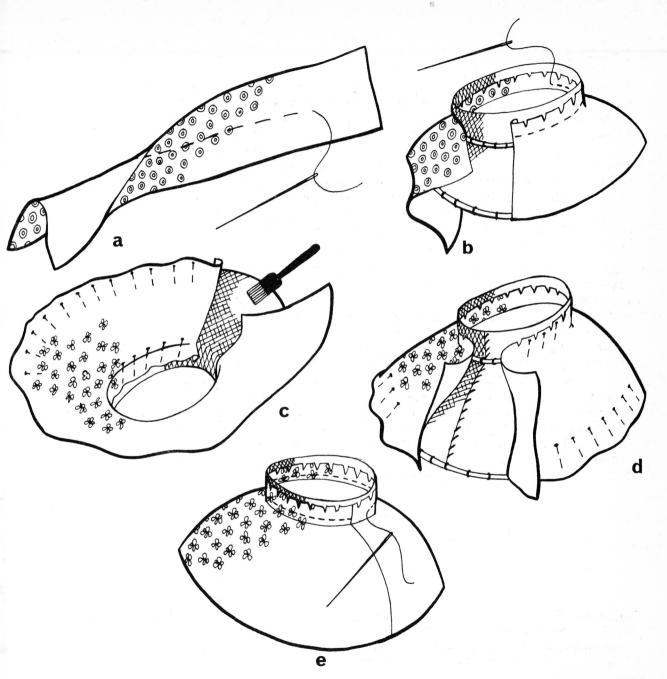

a

b

c

d

e

Figure 21   Brim edge finishes
(a) Edge being slip stitched   (b) Edge being bound   (c) One edge being turned over the other

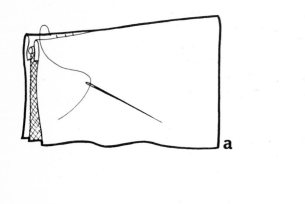

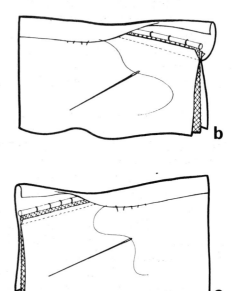

Brim edge finishes   Figure 21 (a),(b),and (c)

The type of finish will depend on the effect required and also upon which is the most suitable method for the fabric.

The easiest way is to turn both brim edges in and slip stitch them neatly together.

If a matching or contrasting binding is used, stitch it, by hand or machine, on to the right side of the brim and slip stitch the other edge on to the wrong side.

Sometimes one side can be cut level with the brim edge and the other side turned over this by about 19 mm ($\frac{3}{4}$ in.). It is turned in again and slip stitched down.

The completed crown and brim are joined by back stitching or stab stitching. Choose the most convenient method but make sure that the stitches do not show on the right side. Attach any trimmings securely. If the hat is very neat on the inside, it might only need a petersham ribbon headband, otherwise a full lining is better.

Section Four   Working in felt

Felt, one of the oldest and most traditional of all millinery fabrics, is not woven like a normal fabric but is made from loose fibres compressed together by many processes to form an extremely varied and useful material. It has no bias like other woven fabrics and can therefore be stretched and steamed in any direction. Its advantages to a milliner are: its extreme pliability, variety of finishes and its ability to take and hold a blocked shape.

The best modern millinery felts are made from fur, usually rabbit. They hold their texture very well and can be re-blocked successfully. The quality of a wool felt depends on the original quality of the sheep's wool used in its manufacture. Over-steaming can cause a wool felt to shrink, so if possible, always use the better quality fur felt.

Both types of felt come in a variety of weights, shapes, colours and finishes. The two most commonly used hood shades are a capeline—a simple crown with a large flat brim and the cone—a large bell shape. An overblown beret shape is sometimes available from millinery suppliers.

A beginner would normally start on a plain hood which has a matt finish and no pile as this would not need such delicate handling as the melusine and peachbloom hoods. The pile of a melusine hood can be extremely varied, long, short or in-between, depending on the type required. A peachbloom has a short velvet-like pile.

When purchasing a hood, remember what it is needed for. It would be wasteful and unnecessary to buy a capeline if you are only going to make a small, close fitting cloche, because a cone would be quite sufficient. Try to handle the hood as little as possible when blocking, particularly peachbloom and melusine types, otherwise the felt might plush, ie, the pile will mark and flatten, this can also be caused by over use of pins.

Stitches

There are certain stitches used only when working in felt. These are darning, oversewing and grafting.

The darning stitch Figure 22 (a) is used for making an 'invisible' edge to edge join, when both sides of the work show simultaneously, eg, an upturned brim. The felt is put together, edge to edge, and stitched diagonally through the thickness about 3·2 mm ($\frac{1}{8}$ in.) either side of the seam. The diagonal stitch means that the stitches are opposite each other along the whole length of the seam. This is not a strong join and should be used where there is little strain.

The oversewing stitch (b) is used for oversewing felt together from the wrong or inside of the join. The right sides are placed together and a neat evenly spaced row of stitching is made along the whole length of the seam, taking the thread through and over the edges of the felt. This is an extremely strong join and is pressed flat when finished.

The grafting stitch (c) is almost the same as the oversewing stitch, except that the felt is put together edge to edge instead of right side to right side. The stitch is worked from the wrong side and passed through the thickness of the felt so that no stitches show on the right side but oversewn stitches appear on the wrong side. Start and finish all stitches with a strong, neat backstitch.

Figure 22 Stitches *(a) Darning (b) Oversewing (c) Grafting*

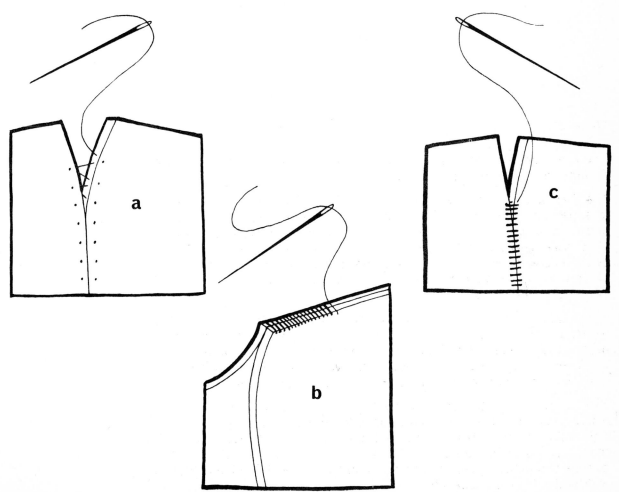

Figure 23   Blocking a felt hood
(a) Felt hood is pinned and steamed   (b) Separating cut is made   (c) Felt brim being steamed over a ring block   (d) Brim edge is wired and finished   (e) Crown and brim are joined together   (f) Finished felt hat with top stitched felt band added for trimming

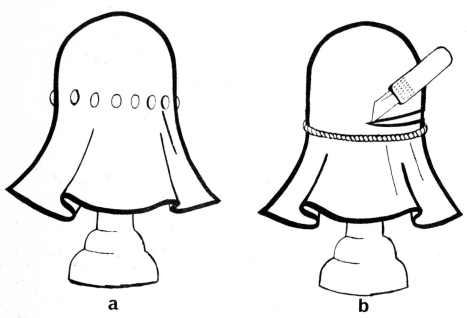

a   b

Blocking a hood   Figure 23 (a) and (b)

Blocking a felt hood is one of the easiest tasks in millinery. Thoroughly soften the hood in steam until it is sufficiently pliable, then stretch it over the block holding it down with drawing pins, or a spiral, at its base. Pin the crown down only as far as is necessary or you might find that you have marked the top part of the brim. Pins and spirals can leave holes and marks, so make sure that they are in positions where any marks made will not show. When the hood has dried mark the centre front of the crown and brim with tailors chalk or cotton then cut off the brim section leaving a clean cut edge and making sure that the bottom of the crown does not stretch while doing so. Wire the edge of the crown with no. 6 wire. This is for support when a brim is to be attached and is removed when the hat is finished.

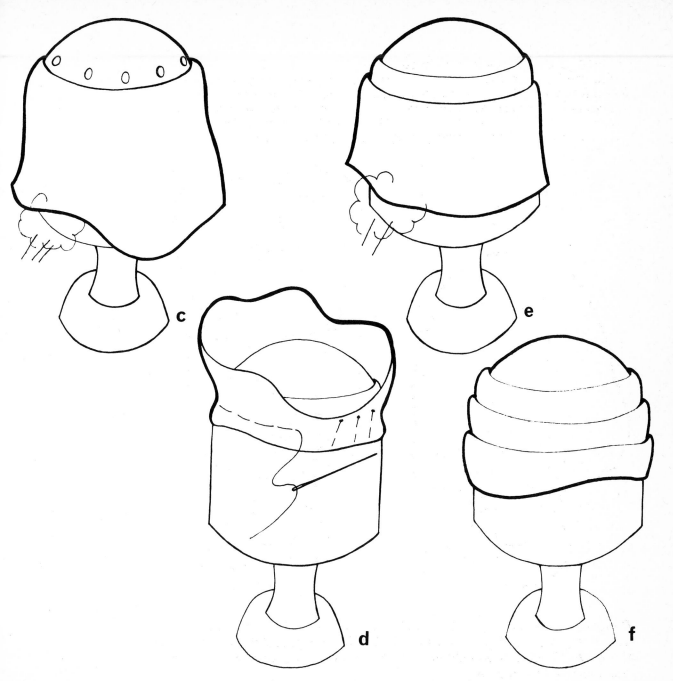

c

d

e

f

Figure 25   Brim edge finishes   *(a) Hemming   (b) Binding   (c) Rolled binding*
(d) Faced edge

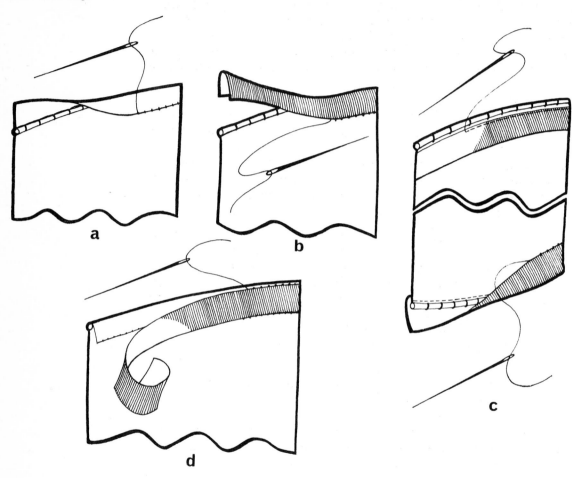

a

b

c

d

Brim edge finishes

The easiest finish of all is to leave the brim with a neatly trimmed raw edge, but this will depend entirely on the shape holding ability of the felt used and the effect required.

Hemming Figure 25 (a) To finish with a hem the edge of the brim is turned approximately 13 mm ($\frac{1}{2}$ in.) over a wire. The wire is necessary initially to get a clean line. If the brim is turned down all the way round, the hem is turned on the inside, but when you have a brim that is partially upturned, then only you as the designer can decide whether you will have the hem on the topside or underside of the brim. Firstly, hold the wire in the required position with a tacking stitch, then permanently sew it in the fold line with a wire stitch—there is no need for the wire stitch if it is to be a narrow hem of less than 13 mm ($\frac{1}{2}$ in.). Turn the hem over, steaming, shrinking and trimming the hem to the width you need—pliers are useful in this operation for pulling the surplus felt away. The hem can then be glued down with millinery solution or hemmed neatly with an upright hemming stitch. If the brim will hold its shape without a wire once the hem has been turned, then tack the wire and remove before finally completing the last 50 to 70 mm (2 to 3 in.) of hemming.

Binding (b) Millinery petersham is folded in half lengthways and then steamed and pressed into a curve, in a similar way to that of a headband, or on a ribbon board if you have one. The brim edge is wired with a wire stitch and the ribbon is then fitted over no. 6 wire and stitched neatly through the grain of both edges all the way round with an upright hemming stitch. At the centre back turn the ribbon under and slip stitch to finish. With this method the wider the ribbon the more necessary it is to make sure that it has been pre-shaped sufficiently to the brim edge.

Rolled binding (c) This is a second way of binding with petersham. Again, almost any width required can be used. The petersham is laid on the topside of the brim, just inside the wired edge and tacked in position. The ends are turned in and slip stitched at the centre back. If it is stretched and tacked too tightly the brim might buckle. Next, backstitch or machine stitch down, remove the tacking, turn over the wired brim edge and then hem the ribbon into position on the underside of the brim by an upright hemming stitch. Press carefully and lightly. This method I find a little more complicated than the flat binding and not quite so successful because of the extra bulk.

Faced edge (d) Wire and make narrow hem, slip stitch the hem into place so that no stitches show on the right side. Curve petersham, again as you would for a headband, the width required and place the longer edge almost to the edge of the brim and tack into position. Sew both edges of the ribbon to the felt with an upright hemming stitch, turn the ends under at the centre back and slip stitch. Remove tacking. This gives an extremely neat finish and appearance to a felt brim.

The brim is attached to the crown, either on the inside or outside of the crown edge, by pinning and then stab stitching into position, working from the centre front markings. A petersham 13 mm ($\frac{1}{2}$ in.) no. 3 curved ribbon is slip stitched in place and any head wire in the crown can then be removed. The hat is now ready for any trimming that is necessary.

Some hoods can be stiff and unyielding and will not respond to steaming very well. If this is the case, thoroughly soak the inside of the hood so that the water can soften up the felt into a more pliable state. It should then respond more normally to steaming.

If any hood has to be stretched a lot, use an egg iron. Heat the iron on a gas ring, put into the clamp, cover with a damp cloth to prevent scorching the inside of the hood, and then pull and stretch the felt into the shape required, repeating until it is sufficient.

Most felt hats are improved if they are steamed lightly and the pile given a final brush with a wire brush for hardy types and a softer brush for peachblooms. If the hat has got soiled slightly while it is being made, a soft detergent or felt cleaner should remove any marks. Use according to the instructions on the labels.

Section Five   Working in straw

If felt could be called the traditional winter hat material, then straw with its tremendous variety of textures and colour is definitely that of the summer. It can be woven into cone and capeline hoods or into braids and plaits of different widths, known as band straw.

The straws have traditionally come from Switzerland, Italy and the Far East, hence some of the exotic names, and have been woven from natural plants and grasses. However many 'straws' nowadays can be wholly or partly synthetic.

Strawcloth or laize   is available by the yard in many colours and designs and can vary in width from 457 mm (18 in.) upwards. It it not always made from straw and can be synthetic. It is normally used for covering foundation shapes but because of its loose weave, has to be handled carefully to stop it from fraying. A line of straw stiffener brushed along the raw edges before the shape is assembled will sometimes help the fraying problem.

Blocking a smooth straw hood

The smooth hand woven straws such as pari-buntal and panamas need extreme care when being blocked and as with all millinery, should be handled as little as possible. They are woven from the centre of the tip to the base and need to be centred carefully before commencing to block.

When blocking a capeline shape, try to leave the crown and brim in one piece. If this is not possible, before separating them, machine two parallel lines about 6·4 mm ($\frac{1}{4}$ in.) apart and cut between these two lines. This will stop the straw unravelling or fraying, which can happen very easily along a cut edge. If you can leave 13 mm ($\frac{1}{2}$ in.) of the bottom of the crown on the brim when you separate the two, this will make it easier for you to join them back together again.

Because the smooth straws can be very unyielding a strong block is needed to cope with the 'brute force' involved when working them. Before steaming over the block, damp the inside of the hood and leave a while as this will help to soften it up before blocking. Pull the hood over the block, ease on the spiral and then pull along the 'grain' of the straw. Steam as for felt. Do not separate crown and brim, if necessary, until this stage has been completed, because the brim is easy to pull and tug when the hood is being steamed over the block.

When it has dried, iron over a dry cloth—this helps to 'set' the shape. Be extremely careful with a Leghorn hood because it will scorch easily. Should it be necessary to press it, use a very cool iron over a dry cloth.

Brims Block a straw brim as for felt, making sure that the head measurements of the brim and crown are approximately the same. If the brim is to be given a lot of shaping and needs cutting, use one of the following methods for rejoining the seam.

Brim joins

Lapped seam *Figure 26* (a) For an upturned brim where both sides of the brim will be showing, use a lapped seam. Overlap the cut edges about 13 mm ($\frac{1}{2}$ in.) and sew together temporarily with a tacking stitch along the centre. Turn the edges in and neatly slip stitch or machine stitch both folded edges to the brim. Remove tacking stitch and lightly press. This seam is also known as an interlocking seam.

Flat seam (b) If the wrong side of a seam is not going to show, the brim can be joined by a flat seam. The edges of the join are placed together right side to right side and machined. The join is pressed open. The turnings are machined down to the brim about 3 mm ($\frac{1}{8}$ in.) either side of the seam and then the surplus turning is neatly cut away. The turnings, instead of being machine stitched, can be turned in and slip stitched.

Brim edge finishes (c), (d) and (e)

The easiest way is to turn the brim edge over a wire, tack down temporarily and then machine right up to the wire using a half foot on the sewing machine. (This foot is normally used for inserting zips or piping cord.) It can also be glued over the wire although this is not very satisfactory because the glue can leave marks. Trim away any excess straw, and remove tacking stitch. This gives an extremely neat finish on the right side of a brim but as some people do not like the raw edge on the inside there is an alternative method. Run a line of machining around the brim edge to stop it from fraying. Turn it over about 6 mm ($\frac{1}{4}$ in.) on the inside of the

Figure 26 Brim joins *(a) Lapped seam   (b) Flat seam*
Brim edge finishes *(c) Raw edge turned over a wire   (d) Raw edge is turned
in and then turned over wire   (e) Crossway binding*

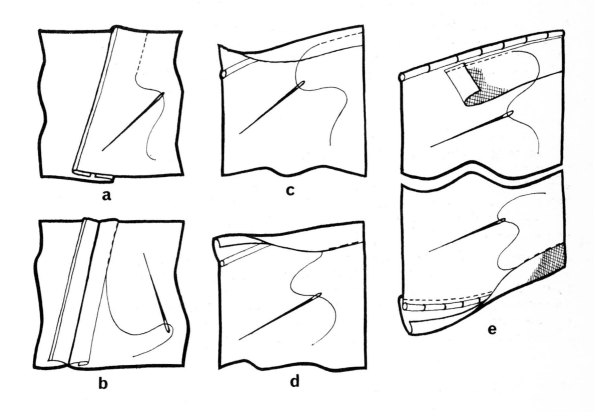

brim and then turn it over again, but this time over a wire. Either machine stitch or slip stitch the folded edge on to the brim and press carefully.

A brim can be most attractively finished with a crossway binding cut from a matching or contrasting fabric. Cut a strip of fabric on the cross the length of the brim edge plus 51 mm (2 in.). The width will depend on the width required for the finished binding but remember that anything less than 32 mm (1¼ in.) will be more difficult to work. Wire the edge of the brim, using a wire stitch and no. 6 wire. Turn one end of the binding over 13 mm (½ in.) and place at the centre back of the brim, right side of the binding to the right side of the brim. If you intend putting a bow or trimming of some kind on the brim edge anywhere other than at the centre back, then you can start the binding there because then the trimming will cover up the join.

Tack the binding down the necessary width away from the brim edge, making sure that it does not stretch, otherwise it will get narrower, and then machine down, taking a 6·4 mm (¼ in.) turning off the binding. Trim off any excess binding at the centre back and remove the tacking stitches. Fold the binding back over the wired edge turning the other side of the binding in 6·4 mm (¼ in.) and slip stitch down to the wrong side of the brim, including the back join.

Joining brims to crowns

If the crown is going to have a trimming which will cover up the join, then slip the brim under the crown and back stitch together. Add the trimming and finish with a no. 3 petersham ribbon which has been curved. If the finished hat is going to remain completely plain where the crown and brim come together, then a different method is used. Turn the edge of the crown under about 13 mm ($\frac{1}{2}$ in.) and slip stitch the fold to the brim which is slipped inside the crown. Finish with a petersham headband. Varnish on the inside with straw stiffener if necessary.

Working with 'rough' straws

Most of these straws fall into the cellophane straw category, which, as its name suggests, is not a true straw. They are extremely pliable and easy to shape, reacting very well to steaming. The most important point to remember when working with these straws is not to press them, otherwise you will flatten and destroy all the surface interest.

Try not to cut them because they unravel easily. If it is unavoidable, run two or three rows of large tacking stitches around the crown using the natural weave of the fabric. *Sellotape* will also stop the weave from unravelling.

Figure 27　*(a) Straw crown being steamed over block　(b) Wire being inserted into the fold of a brimless straw hat　(c) Petersham headband being inserted*

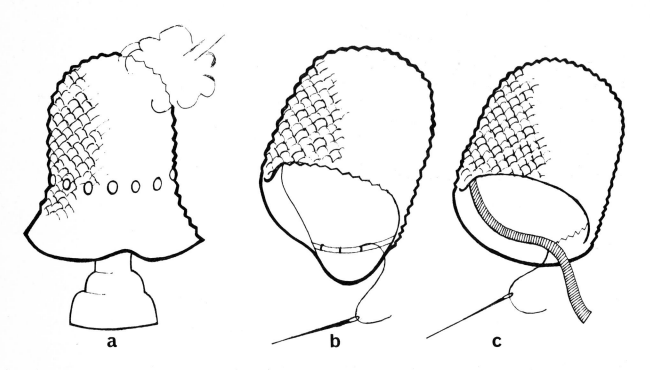

a　　　　　　　　b　　　　　　　　c

Crowns　Figure 27 (a), (b) and (c)

Steam the straw over the block holding it down with drawing pins placed in between the weave to stop the straw from splitting. Do not use a spiral unless it is in a position that will not show, because the tension will flatten the surface and leave a mark. When it is completely dry, remove from the block, fold the bottom inside and insert a wire into the fold with a stab stitch making the stitches as invisible as possible. Make sure that the part that has been folded over does not cause the bottom of the crown to bulge out slightly—if it does, steam and manipulate away by hand. Stiffen the inside with a straw stiffener and insert a petersham headband.

　Straw stiffener should only be used when the hat is completely dry, otherwise the surface can 'blister'.

Figure 27 *(d) Brim edge being finished by a crossway strip of fabric*

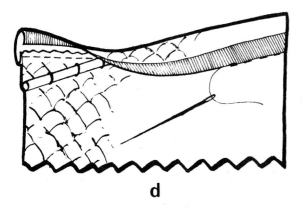

d

Brims (d)

Steam and pin the brim over the block as for the crown. It is best to use the natural edge of the brim for finishing the edge if it is at all possible. Turn the edge over a wire and stitch down, taking advantage of the weave to hide the stitches. Alternatively, if the edge has to be cut, machine a narrow crossway binding along the edge, right sides together, and then turn the straw over a wire. Stitch the wire into the fold, turn the binding in 6 mm ($\frac{1}{4}$ in.) and slip stitch to the underbrim. To stop the head fitting from stretching too much, a temporary wire can be fitted and then removed after the brim and crown have been joined together.

Attach the brim to the crown by the same methods as for a smooth straw, except that it is better to fold the crown edge over a wire if it is going to be an untrimmed hat. This gives a clean line. Varnish if needed when it is completely finished, and on no account press or steam again, otherwise it will ruin the straw.

69

Figure 28 Band straws
(a) The beginning of a spiralled crown   (b) Band straw being attached to a leno base

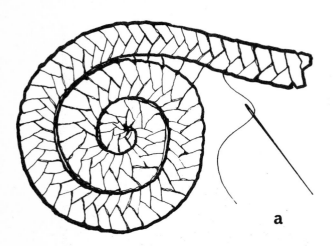

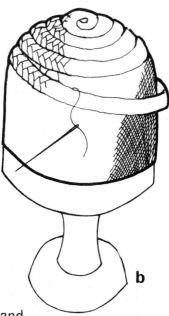

a

b

Working with band straw   Figure 28 (a), (b), (c), (d) and (e)

Band straw comes in a bewildering variety of textures, colours and widths, and is sold in packets or by the yard. If it is to be made into a complicated crown or a large brim, then a leno or dior net foundation shape will be necessary for support. It can be made up with no foundation shape at all if it is not too large or exaggerated a shape. When working with band straws it is still necessary to manipulate and shape them in steam. To start the shape, first oversew the end of the braid to stop it from unravelling. If there is a thread running through the middle of the band straw, pull it up to form the straw into a circle. From this circle coil the band round so that the edges interlock or overlap neatly together, depending upon the effect required. You can pin the straw into position on the block before stab stitching the bands together with thread or fine raffia. Hide the stitches carefully among the weave—the eye of a needle is best for this job as the sharp end can cause the straw to split. Arrange the coiling so that the last band can be tucked under the headline at the centre back. An alternative method is to stitch the straw on to a net foundation shape or to work the straw completely in the hand, though this will only come with experience and practice.

Figure 28 *(c) Interweaving band straw together   (d) Spiralling band straw round a brim   (e) Covering a brim with strips of band straw that are joined together by interweaving*

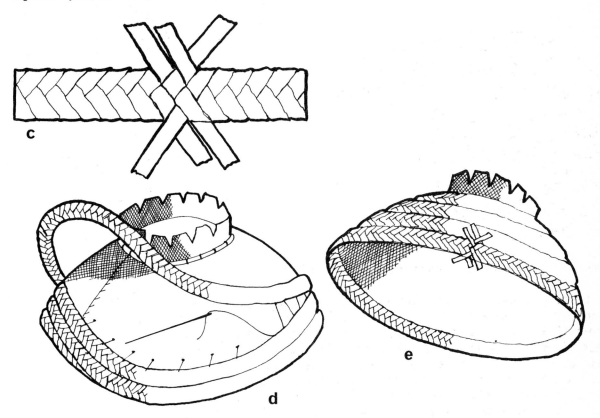

To make the brim start from the outer edge about 76 mm (3 in.) left of the centre back, looking at the brim from the back. The straw is then spiralled round and stitched like the crown until the headline is reached, where it is joined to the bottom of the crown. With a plaited braid, the brim can be worked in separate pieces rather than a continuous piece. This, if at all possible, gives a much better effect and finish. Pin the lengths to the brim block, leaving a 51 mm (2 in.) overlap at the centre back. Both ends can be unplaited and then replaited carefully together, so that no join is visible. Interlock or overlap the bands as required and stitch together.

With a large picture brim, mount the straw on a similar coloured dior net which has been wired at the brim edge and then stitch another band of straw on the underside of the brim covering the wire completely. This method of finishing a brim edge can be used even if there is no foundation shape. Wire 13 mm ($\frac{1}{2}$ in.) inside the edge of the underside of the brim and then stitch the underband on. If you think that the underside of the brim looks unsightly with some of the stitches showing it can be lined with a matching or contrasting lightweight fabric, as explained in Section Three. I think that this is defeating the beauty and quality of any straw hat and I would rather recommend neater and more careful workmanship making a lining unnecessary.

Joining crowns and brims

The crown and brim can be joined edge to edge or the crown can slip over the brim. In both cases stab stitch together as invisibly as possible. Finish the inside of the crown and underside of the brim with a coat of straw stiffener—this will help to hold the shape. Insert a 13 mm ($\frac{1}{2}$ in.) curved petersham, cut to the correct size, for the head fitting.

Pedal Straw   Figure 29 (a), (b), (c) and (d)

This is a four or five stranded and stitched band straw, and is difficult to work for a beginner. It can be rather tough and might need constant dampening and pressing to soften it into a manageable form.

Unpick one of the edge rows about 150 mm (6 in.) and coil round as for a band straw stitching together. Cut off next row, unpick for about 102 mm (4 in.). Slip cut end under coiled straw and spiral round. Repeat with the other rows until the full width of the band can be easily steamed and manipulated around to form the desired shape. To finish off the crown unpick the rows and cut in a stepped manner tucking the rows under the finished bands.

Figure 29   *(a), (b), (c) and (d) Starting and joining in the various strands of a pedal straw*

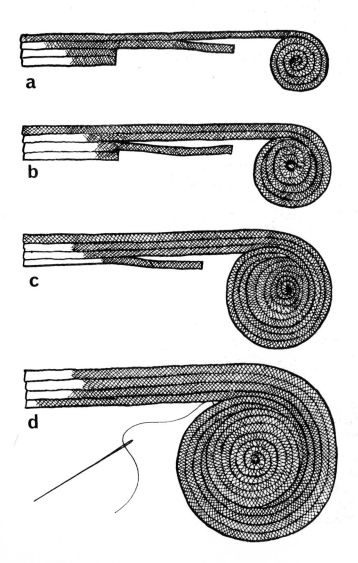

Figure 29 *(e) Starting a pedal straw which is to be spiralled round a brim (f) Interweaving the strands of a pedal straw for a neat join*

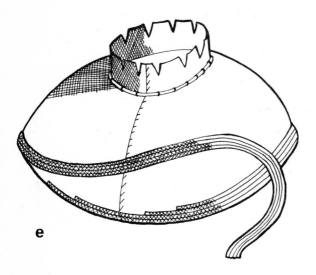

e

f

For the brim, *Figure 29 (e) and (f),* work from the brim edge to the headline. Unpick and step out the rows, placing the middle row at the centre back of the brim. Spiral the band round covering up the cut ends at the beginning. Steam and press the bands into the required shape if the straw will not handle easily. Finish off as the bottom of the crown.

To finish stitch crown and brim together, varnish and put in head ribbon.

Because of the great variety of straws and the different ways of working each one, there can be various methods of dealing with the same problem, depending on the effect required. Practice and commonsense will solve most of the problems which might arise.

Section Six Flat pattern hats

This is the method by which it is possible to make hats without any blocks at all. It is very useful for using up odd lengths of materials and normal dressmaking procedures are generally followed. Any fabric can be used although care must be taken with fabrics that have a one way design or pile, eg, velvet, corduroy. When using a striped or checked fabric, try to match the lines—as the sections are usually cut on the bias, interesting diagonal patterns can be produced. The fabric is mounted on a base; leno, tarlatan, foam and lawn can be used, depending upon how much 'body' is needed in the hat, and both sections are machined together. Flat pattern hats lend themselves particularly to top stitching—the pattern pieces are easy to machine and the rows of stitching give extra stiffening. All measurements must be extremely accurate, especially when machining turnings, otherwise it is easy to make the hat too large or too small. The methods for shaping brims can be adapted for spartre foundation shapes and coverings very easily.

Brims

The shape of a brim can range from a perfectly flat boater shape to a deep close-fitting cloche. There can be tremendous variation between these two extremes. There are two basic and very easy methods of making a brim pattern. With one, a rectangular piece of paper is cut and opened out to give extra width at the brim edge. Alternatively, a circular piece of paper is darted and closed to make the brim edge smaller. Either of these methods will enable most brims to be constructed from a flat pattern. Any reasonably firm, large piece of paper that will not tear easily will be suitable for drafting the pattern; brown wrapping paper is excellent.

Method 1   Figure 30 (a), (b), (c), (d) and (e)   Cut a rectangular piece of paper the length of the head measurement plus 25 mm (1 in.) for turnings. The width will be the widest part of the brim plus 25 mm (1 in.) for turning. Fold a line along its length 25 mm (1 in.) inside an edge—this indicates the headfitting line and turning. Divide the paper into 25 mm (1 in.) sections across its width. From the edge that is to become the brim edge, cut along these lines as far as the headfitting line. Overlap the two edges 13 mm ($\frac{1}{2}$ in.) —this will be the centre back of the brim—and form the headband into an oval shape approximately 25 mm (1 in.) longer than it will be wide. The strips will hang down to form a tube but if the tube is lowered on to a flat surface they will be flat like the spokes of a wheel. The shape of the brim will be somewhere between these two points. Carefully pin the paper to a dummy head or crown block and then decide upon the angle and type of brim that is needed. Use *Sellotape* or gummed paper to hold the strips together into the shape that is required. When you have an overall shape with which you are satisfied, trim the brim edge to the proper width. Generally the back width is about 25 mm (1 in.) narrower than the front and the sides a little wider than the front. This is to achieve a balanced look but it will depend upon the design.

Cut through the centre back and pin the brim flat on to another piece of paper. Mark round the brim edge, back seam and headfitting line. Remove the old pattern and even out any crooked lines to form a clean brim edge. Add 13 mm ($\frac{1}{2}$ in.) turning to the back seam and brim edge and a 19 mm ($\frac{3}{4}$ in.) turning to the headfitting line. Mark in the centre front, centre sides, grain of fabric, the bias usually runs through the centre front and any other relevant information necessary for constructing the brim.

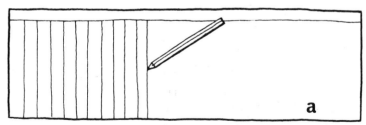

Figure 30   Brims, Method 1
(a) Marking up the pattern   (b) Cutting the strips   (c) Deciding the shape of the brim on a dummy head   (d) Transferring the shape to the final pattern paper (e) Cutting out the final pattern, to which allowances have been made

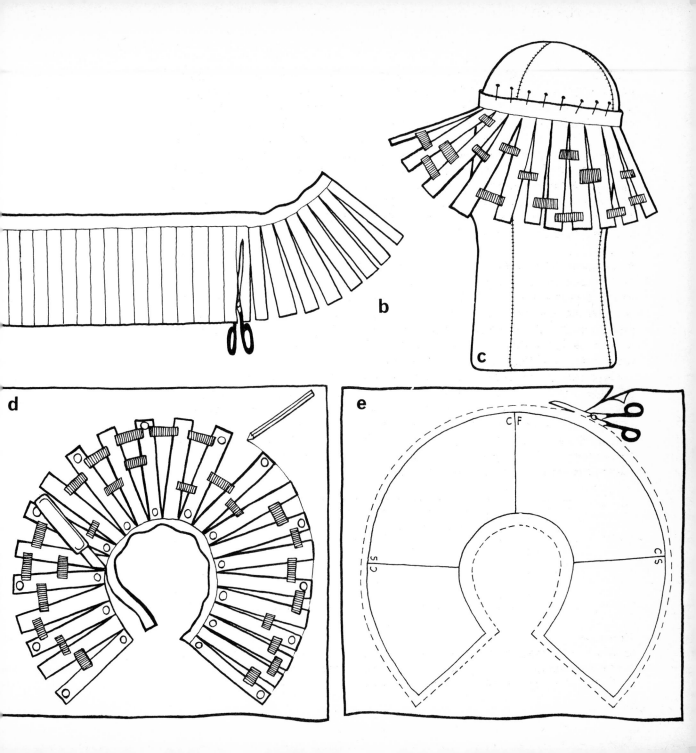

b

c

d

e

Method 2 Figure 31 (a), (b), (c) and (d) This is almost the reverse of the previous method. Instead of a tubular shape being cut and spread open, a flat circular shape is darted, or cut, and closed up.

On a large sheet of paper, draw two lines, approximately 508 mm (20 in.) long, crossing each other in the middle at right angles. Mark off 13 mm (½ in.) measurements on each line, starting at the point at which they cross, for about 102 to 127 mm (4 to 5 in.). Take the head measurement and place the tape measure on to the paper to form an oval 25 mm (1 in.) longer than it is wide—using the 13 mm (½ in.) measurements as guidelines. The longer measurement is placed so that it runs through the oval from the centre front to the centre back. Make the oval symmetrical either side of this line. Trace lightly round the tape measure and then remove the tape so that the oval can be checked visually to see that it is evenly balanced. Re-measure and if correct, re-draw the headfitting line. If the measurement is a little bit out, a line drawn 3 mm (⅛ in.) outside or inside the original fitting line will add or subtract 13 mm (½ in.) to the measurement of the fitting line. Draw a line 25 mm (1 in.) inside the final headfitting line for a turning and cut out the oval that is left. From the headfitting line measure out to the proposed brim edge using the two long lines as guidelines for the centre front, centre back and centre side measurements. Draw the brim edge shape approximately and cut away the surplus paper. Cut the headline turning every 25 mm (1 in.) up to the headfitting line and pin the cut turning on to a strong paper headband cut to the head measurement. The resultant brim shape will be a completely flat boater.

To make a deep slanted brim, the hat shape must be darted sufficiently to reduce the brim edge and bring it in closer to the head. Make small darts where they are needed to slant the brim (it does not have to be symmetrical all round) making sure that they are tapered out at the headfitting line. This is so that the headline does not get reduced in measurement. The darts can be *Sellotaped* into place.

Figure 31   Brims, Method 2
(a) Marking up the pattern   (b) Deciding the shape of the brim

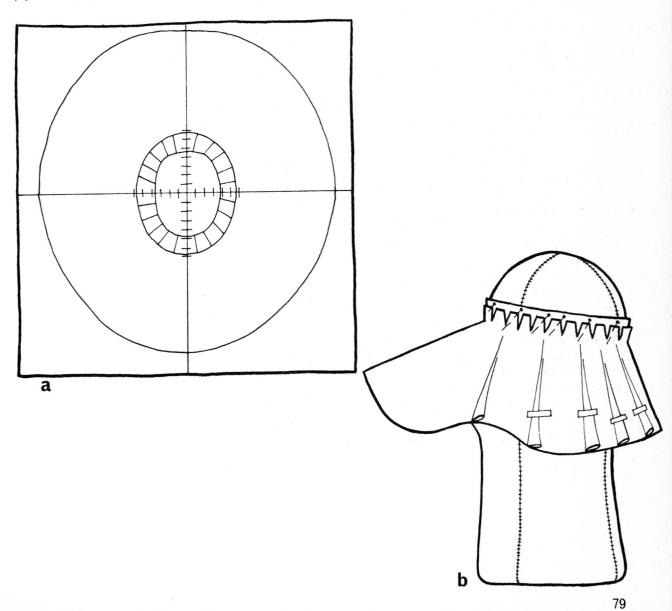

a

b

Figure 31 *(c) Transferring the shape to the final pattern*
(d) Cutting the final pattern, to which allowances
have been made

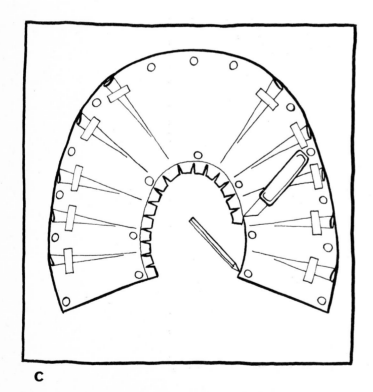

c

When the brim shaping has been finished re-draw the brim edge which has probably become distorted. Cut through the centre back and cut away the head turning at the head line. Put the darted pattern on to a fresh sheet of paper and draw accurately around the shape for the final pattern. Add 13 mm ($\frac{1}{2}$ in.) turnings to the centre back seam and brim edge and 19 mm ($\frac{3}{4}$ in.) turning to the headline. Mark in the centre front and any other guidelines that might help when the brim is to be made up. Although both these methods sound complicated, they are extremely easy to do, and with a little practice almost any brim shape can be developed.

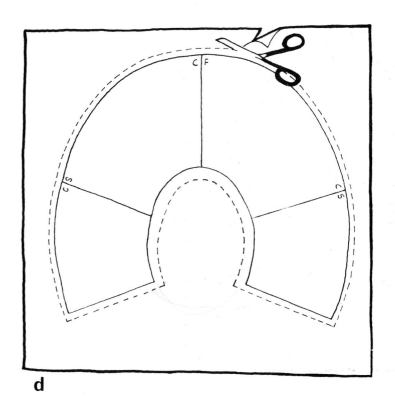

d

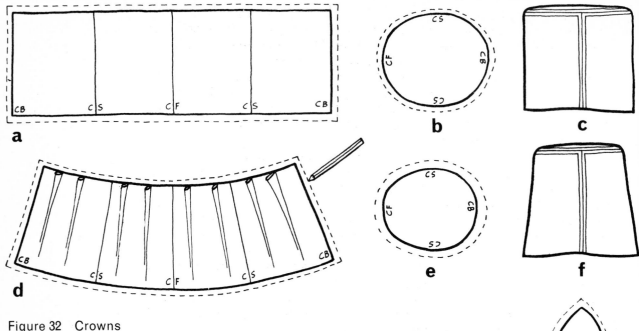

Figure 32 Crowns
(a) Marking up sideband (b) Marking up tip (c) Stovepipe shape of crown which this pattern will give (d) Marking up sideband (e) Marking up tip (f) Flowerpot shape of crown which this pattern will give (g) and (h) Panel with resultant crown shape (i) and (j) Panel with resultant crown shape

Crowns

Can be made either by the tip and sideband method or in sections. *Figure 32 (a), (b), (c), (d), (e), (f), (g), (h), (i) and (j).*

Tip and sideband The simplest way of making a tip and sideband crown is to have a plain unshaped sideband. The width of the sideband is the required crown depth plus 13 mm ($\frac{1}{2}$ in.) turnings either side for joining it to the tip and brim. The length will be the headfitting measurement plus 25 mm (1 in.) for back seam turnings. Cut this shape out of stiff paper and pin the back seam together. Form this 'tube' shape into an oval 25 mm (1 in.) longer than it is wide and place it firmly on to another sheet of paper.

Using this as a guide, draw a line round the bottom edge of the 'tube' on to the paper. Evenly cut the line so that it forms a well balanced oval and add 13 mm ($\frac{1}{2}$ in.) all round for turnings. This will be the tip and when it is joined to the sideband it will form a plain 'stovepipe' crown.

A 'flowerpot' style crown, where the top of the crown is smaller than the base, is made in a similar way, except that the sideband is shaped. Measure and cut the sideband as before but do not add any turnings. Next, take out a number of darts to reduce the top edge. The darts can be folded out or cut down almost to the bottom edge and overlapped about 6 mm ($\frac{1}{4}$ in.) at the top edge. A lot of smaller darts will give a smoother, better curve than fewer, larger ones, so make them no larger than 13 mm ($\frac{1}{2}$ in.). The number of darts will depend upon how narrow the crown is needed at the top. When the shape has been decided upon, pin the pattern to a fresh sheet of paper. Add 13 mm ($\frac{1}{2}$ in.) all round for the turnings and the back seam and cut out. Make the tip as before, but add 16 to 19 mm ($\frac{5}{8}$ to $\frac{3}{4}$ in.) turning. This is because the actual top edge of the sideband is smaller than the point at which the seam is taken, and if an allowance is not made for this, the tip could be too small.

When making a tip and sideband crown, mark in the centre front, centre back and centre side points on both sections as this will make it much easier when joining them together.

Sectional crown   The shape and number of the sections will depend upon the style of the crown. The most important point to remember is extreme accuracy in making the pattern and in stitching the sections together. A sectional crown is normally made from six identical sections although it can be more or less. The base of a section will be the head measurement, divided by the number of sections, eg on the six-sectional crown for a 572 mm (22$\frac{1}{2}$ in.) head, the measurement will be 95 mm (3$\frac{3}{4}$ in.). The height of the section will depend upon the height of the crown, allowing for the curvature to the centre where all the sections will meet. The shape of the crown will depend upon the shape of the sections and this can only be learnt by trial and error as there are no other specific measurements to be taken. For instance, if you want the crown to be bulbous at some point, then the section will have to measure wider at a certain point than it is at the base. If you want the crown to be the same all the way up, then keep the sides of each section parallel. You will have to use your imagination to judge what the crown is going to look like when all the sections have been joined together.

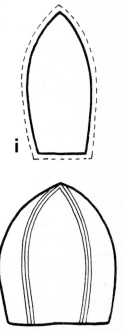

Figure 33 (a) Laying up the pattern pieces (b) Tacking the outer and base fabric together (c) Assembling the crown sections (d) Finished crown where seams have been top stitched

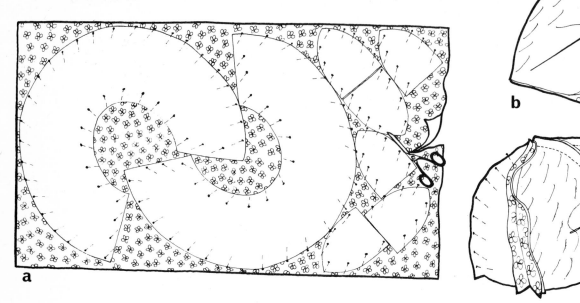

a

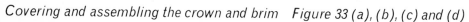
b

c

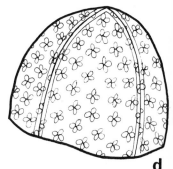
d

Covering and assembling the crown and brim Figure 33 (a), (b), (c) and (d)

Lay the pattern pieces on the fabric, making sure that those needing to be cut on the bias are correctly placed. Interlock them so that they can be cut in the most economical way, paying particular attention to the matching of any pattern, and the direction of any pile. Choose a base or interlining for your fabric, eg leno, tarlatan, foam, heavy cotton, *Vilene*, etc. and cut out the necessary number of pattern pieces. The lighter the fabric, the lighter will be its base. Tack each piece of covering fabric on to the appropriate section of base material. Machine the crown pieces together. If it is a top stitched, sectioned crown, do the top stitching first as it will be easier than trying to do it when the crown is in one piece. The stitching must be extremely accurate and if the correct turnings are not taken the crown will become smaller or larger. When making a line of top stitching either side of a seam, it is done after the seam has been machined together.

84

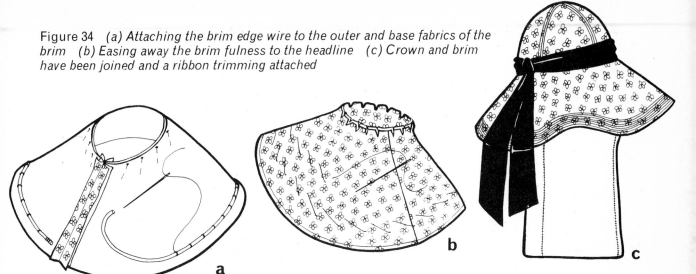

Figure 34 *(a) Attaching the brim edge wire to the outer and base fabrics of the brim (b) Easing away the brim fulness to the headline (c) Crown and brim have been joined and a ribbon trimming attached*

a

b

c

For the brim, *Figure 34 (a), (b) and (c)*, machine the back seams of each section and press them open. Put the right sides of the top and underbrim together and machine round the brim edge, taking the required turning. Extra stiffening can be given to the brim edge by adding a fine wire and this will hold in a particular shape or fold. Stitch the wire along the machine line on the underside of the top brim, attaching it to the interlining so that no stitches will show on the brim edge. Fold the bottom brim under the top brim and tack them firmly together easing any fulness towards the headfitting line. The brim can be top stitched or given any other decorative treatment.

The bottom of the crown is turned under 13 mm ($\frac{1}{2}$ in.) and pinned to the headfitting line of the brim. Match the centre front, centre back, and centre side of the crown and brim and then evenly distribute any slight fulness before slip stitching them together. Add a lining and 13 mm ($\frac{1}{2}$ in.) curved petersham to finish off neatly.

The hat can be made reversible by making two crowns and slip stitching the second 'inside' the first in place of a lining. If you do this use your own judgment as to whether the second crown will need an interlining or not—it will depend upon the fabric.

I have mentioned that flat paper patterns are very useful for making spartre or leno brim shapes. If this is done, they are covered by the normal methods for foundation materials. See Section Three.

Berets

As well as being steamed and blocked, berets can be made by a number of flat pattern methods. The simplest of these is the two-part beret.

Two-part beret   Figure 35 (a), (b), (c) and (d) Draw two large circles on to the pattern paper. The diameter of these will depend upon the width required for the beret. In each of the circles make a dart, starting it at the circumference and fading it out at the centre. To make the 'underbrim' section, Sellotape one of the darts securely and make an oval in the circle using the circle centrepoint as the centrepoint of the oval. This is for the headfitting line and so its circumference will be the fitting required.

Undo the dart and cut out the surplus 'keyhole' shape. Place the 'underbrim' on to a fresh sheet of paper, trace round and then add 13 mm (½ in.) turnings on to the headfitting line, back seam and outside edge. Add 13 mm (½ in.) turning to the outside edge of the tip section and mark the position of the dart. To make up, machine the back seam of the under-section and the dart of the tip (if the dart is rather bulky it can be trimmed down after machining). Put the right sides of the sections together, machine round the edges and then turn it through. The headfitting can be finished by inserting a shaped 25 mm (1 in.) wide petersham ribbon. This ribbon is used rather than the more usual 13 mm (½ in.) because it will give extra support.

Alternatively, cut a strip of fabric on the bias 76 mm (3 in.) wide by the headfitting measurement and machine the ends together with a 13 mm (½ in.) seam. No seam allowance is given for this band because being cut on the cross it will easily fit on to the headfitting line. Place the seam of the headband to the seam of the undersection, right sides together, and evenly pin the headband and crown edge together. Machine with a 13 mm (½ in.) seam and turn the headband over the seam and slip stitch the edge down carefully to the seamline turning the raw edge in beforehand.

By altering the size of the circles and taking out different amounts from the darts the size and shape of the beret can be altered. Another variation which will give more scope for design is to insert a crossway strip of fabric between the two sections. This can be of different widths, contrasting colours or patterns, varying textures or even have piping inserted between the seams.

Figure 35   Beret
(a) Laying up and cutting out the pattern   (b) Assembling the sections
(c) Inserting the headband   (d) Finished beret

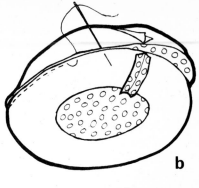

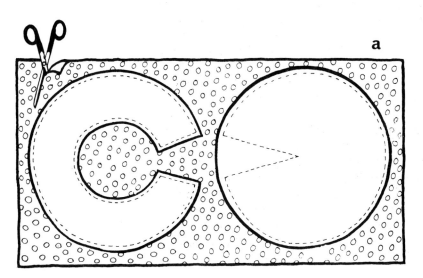

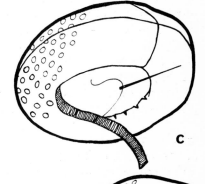

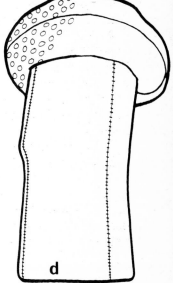

Sectional beret   This is made in a very similar manner to the sectional crown pattern already mentioned. It is important to keep the shape as a smooth, regular silhouette and the more sections that there are, the easier this will be to obtain. Make the sections as for a sectional crown, remembering that they are likely to be wider because of the greater circumference of most berets although this will depend upon whether it is a tailored or a floppy styled beret. You will need to measure the headfitting (divided by the number of sections), the depth of the section from base to tip and the widest part of the circumference, again divided by the number of sections. These measurements will give the approximate shape of one section. A trial beret can be made from muslin or scrap fabric so that the shape of the section can be refined and altered as necessary for the final shape. It is put together like a sectional crown and finished with a headband by one of the beret headband methods.

With imagination it is possible to combine both beret methods and evolve lively and original variations.

Section Seven Trimmings

The addition of a trimming can add an extra touch of originality and individuality to any hat. The choice of a trimming can improve or absolutely ruin what might be a good basic shape. With a little imagination almost anything can be used, eg Easter bonnets, and for this reason it is impossible to enumerate every one. Use of the imagination and a willingness to experiment is the advice I would give to any millinery student who is prepared to be a little bit different.

Ribbons   There is an amazing variety of ribbons to be found in most department stores but the one used most often in millinery is petersham. It comes in many widths and colours and is generally used on very tailored hats as a plain band or flat bow.

Headband   If the sides of the crown are not quite parallel when making a hatband, the ribbon will need to be curved slightly to prevent it from gaping. To do this, stretch one side slightly while pressing the ribbon under a damp cloth with a fairly warm iron. Turn in the ends at the centre back, or under a bow if there is one, and slip stitch them together before slip stitching the ribbon to the crown.

Bows   Figure 36 (a), (b) and (c)   The flat or tailored petersham bow is made by folding two large loops to meet at the centre. This is covered by a plain separate tie. The bow can have ends, separately or joined, which can be trimmed in a slanting or V-shaped manner. To give this bow a softer effect it can be pleated.
   Petersham can easily be pleated and folded to form decorative headbands and brim edges. Keep the pleating crisp and sharp to avoid any feeling of clumsiness. A rosette can be made by forming single pleating into a circle and covering the centre with a self-covered button. When stitching petersham ribbon, sink the thread into the grain and make the stitches as unobtrusive as possible, *(d), (e) and (f)*.
   When using other types of ribbon such as satin, velvet, organdie, etc see that it has as much body in it as possible so that it does not appear limp and lifeless. Ribbon wire placed along the centre of two pieces of ribbon which are glued together is excellent for keeping the shape of a bow, especially if it has long fly-away ends. Leno can also be placed between a double ribbon in the same manner. If a ribbon is transparent,

such as organdie or crystal organza, try stiffening it first with a good straw stiffener. Do this two or three times if necessary, making sure that it does not mark or stain.

With bows, keep practising and experimenting with various types of ribbon until you can easily tie a variety of bows quickly and efficiently. Do not labour and fiddle over a bow, press the ribbon flat and try again.

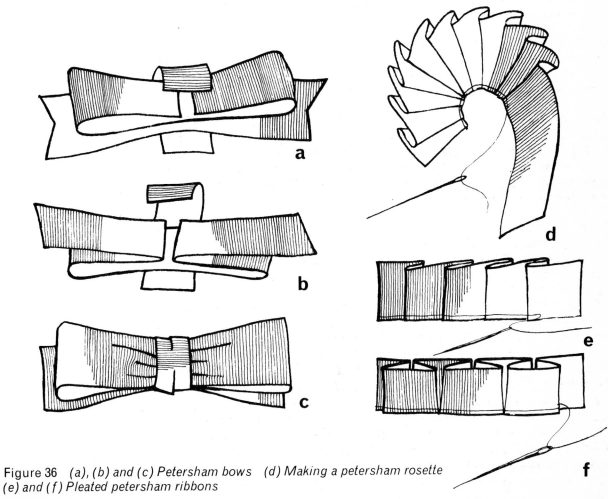

Figure 36 *(a), (b) and (c) Petersham bows* *(d) Making a petersham rosette* *(e) and (f) Pleated petersham ribbons*

Flowers can be used singly or to cover the whole of a hat. Most department stores carry a variety but they can be expensive if a lot of them are needed. The flowers that I will explain how to make are used mainly for completely covering hats. For one lush, extravagant flower that is to be a feature of a hat, it is probably best to buy it.

Petalled flowers Figure 37 (a), (b), (c), (d), (e) and (f). Most materials that are used for making the flowers tend to be fine and delicate, and will have to be stiffened before they are suitable for use. Give the material two or three coats of a clear varnish (straw stiffener) until it has enough body to remain rigid when cut into small shapes. Make sure that it is dry between each application. Alternatively, if the material is of a heavier weight eg, linen, cotton, it can be starched with a proprietary starch, following the given instructions.

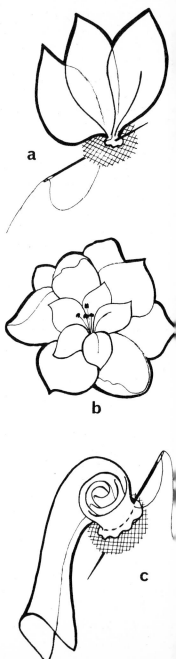

a

b

c

Decide on the shape and size of the petals and cut them out of card. Place the card patterns on to the fabric, with the cross grain running through the centre of the petal, and trace off as many petals as are needed —the stiffening should stop the edges from fraying. Take three or four of the smallest petals and pleat the bottom of each one so that it makes the petal stand up. Bunch these together round a few stamens (these can be bought) and stitch them on to a small circle of leno, about 25 mm (1 in.) diameter for a small flower. Shape the other petals by rolling and stretching the edges, pleat the bottoms and arrange them around the centre of the flower. Stitch them to the leno until you have a shape with which you are satisfied. When enough of the flowers have been made, place them on to the shape and stitch finally into position. This method can make very exciting felt flowers.

Flowers can also be made from a continuous strip of bias cut fabric— organza, chiffon and silk are excellent. The strip is folded along its length and one end attached to a circle of leno—its size will depend upon the size of the flower. The strip is spiralled round and stitched to the leno base. Tuck the end under to finish. When spiralling, do not pull too tightly, otherwise the flower can look too mean.

Petal hats These can be made from single petals cut in the same manner as those used for making flowers.

Another method of forming petals is to make them double, using organdie and a transparent fabric such as chiffon. Machine them together using card petals, cut to the required shape, as a pattern. Leave the bottom unstitched. Trim the fabric very close to the stitching line, turn the petal through the unstitched opening and press.

About four to five dozen petals will probably be needed although this will depend upon their size and also the size of the hat. Cover the foundation shape with the petals in the manner described in Section Three.

These methods of flower making are not meant to produce realistic flowers, they will only give stylised variations. If a realistic flower is needed, department stores offer a great variety in many colours, shapes and sizes.

Feathers Feathers can be bought singly or as mounts. The single feather such as pheasant, osprey, ostrich, cock, etc, is usually the main feature of a hat. Stab stitch them through their quills on to the hat in the minimum number of places necessary to hold them in position. Mounts are made from a group of feathers already fixed to a base—usually net. These are generally used to completely cover a hat. Overlap the feathers so that there are no gaps and stitch or glue the mounts, with rubber solution, on to the foundation shape.

Jewellery Under this loose term can be actual pieces of jewellery, such as brooches or chains, as well as semi-precious stones, beads and sequins which are sewn on to the hat individually. They can all look very effective on dressy cocktail type hats, but wherever the jewellery is placed do not let it look too heavy or clumsy for the shape. Hats can be embroidered with beads and sequins after the foundation shape has been covered or the fabric can be worked separately beforehand and then fitted on to the foundation shape. Buckles and buttons, jewelled or plain, can make excellent trimmings.

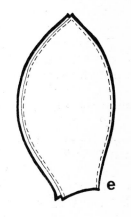

Veiling If the veiling is to fall over the face it will first need to be steamed and shaped on the block. Gather the veiling into the crown of the hat and when it is dry stiffen the net with varnish if needed. Stitch the veiling inside the crown of the hat, at the headfitting and trim away any excess as neatly as possible. If the veiling is swathed round the crown or brim, be generous with it, but do not pull too tightly, especially when stitching it into place.

Figure 37 *(a) Single-thickness starched fabric petals being attached to a leno base (b) Flower completed with bought stamen bunches (c) Crossway strip being spiralled round and attached to a leno base (d) Finished flower (e) Double petal (f) Double petal turned through*

Figure 38   *Examples of top stitching*

Top Stitching   Figure 38.   Although I regard trimmings as 'extras' which are generally put on to a hat when it is almost finished, top stitching, because of its decorative appeal can also be regarded as a trimming. It is normally done while the hat is in the process of being made so plan where the top stitching is to be placed and at what stage it needs to be done before starting the hat.

It can be rows of parallel stitching following the brim of the hat or formed into panels on the brim or the crown. When stitching parallel rows, they look better if they are machined and finished individually rather than one large spiral. Start the stitching at the centre back and finish it neatly by tying a knot underneath the brim or weaving the loose ends into the stitches at the beginning of the row. The thread can be contrasting or matching, but use a slightly darker tone if matching otherwise nothing will show at all. Use a thicker thread, double if necessary, keep the stitches even and make sure that the rows are equally spaced—the width of the machine foot is a good guide. Top stitching will give more body to a hat and look very good on felts. Top stitched felt bands and bows are most effective. *Lurex* thread used on a dark background can look very exciting especially on cocktail type hats. Heavy embroidery thread and buttonhole twist will give added depth to top stitching.

Section Eight   Basic blockmaking

This is the process by which it is possible to make extremely original blocks by reinforcing spartre shapes and hardening them with a stiffening agent. *Figures 39 and 40*.

A crown is reinforced on the inside but a brim can be reinforced on either side, depending upon what type of shape is to be blocked. This fact must be considered before wiring and strengthening the brim otherwise the layers of reinforcement can considerably reduce the size of the head measurement.

Make a spartre shape by the methods, or combination of the methods explained in Section Three, but use the thick no. 90 wire instead of the finer varieties. It might be necessary to take part of the shape from one block, part from another and to mould the rest of the shape in the hands. This is where an egg iron is most useful. The iron is heated in a gas flame, clamped into a stand, the heated part covered with a damp cloth to prevent scorching. By pulling and manipulating the spartre over the iron, curves and shaping that would otherwise prove difficult to work can be set in. Try to make the spartre shape as smooth as possible with the minimum of joins. As the foundation shapes of future hats will depend upon this basic block, it is worthwhile taking a great deal of time and trouble over its making. If there is any section which will come under extra strain and tension when it is being used as a block, reinforce this part with extra wire. When the shape is satisfactory, stiffen it with straw stiffener before reinforcing it by a process known as tabbing.

Spartre strips are cut on the bias about 50 mm (2 in.) wide and 76 to 102 mm (3 to 4 in.) in length to form tabs—although if you are tabbing a large expanse they can be much longer. Never throw away odd shapes of spartre because this is where they become most useful. Dampen the tabs, mould them into the shape and stab stitch them down. When they have dried, repeat—two or three layers should be sufficient for most blocks.

When reinforcement has been completed cut a square of muslin or leno large enough to cover the shape. Steam this over the shape, catch into place any folds or curves by a long stitch and bind the edge of the block with leno. This will help to give it a smooth surface.

Brush the inside and outside of the block evenly with a coat of spartalac —this is the stiffening agent, and stand it upright to dry. After it has dried, it might need to be left overnight, sandpaper any uneven surface and apply a second coat of spartalac. Repeat again if necessary. Clean out the brushes that have been used for the spartalac with a thinning agent, otherwise they will go hard and be completely useless the next time that they are needed.

When the block is being used, always use pins for blocking. Drawing pins can destroy the surface of a spartre block very quickly and are therefore unsuitable.

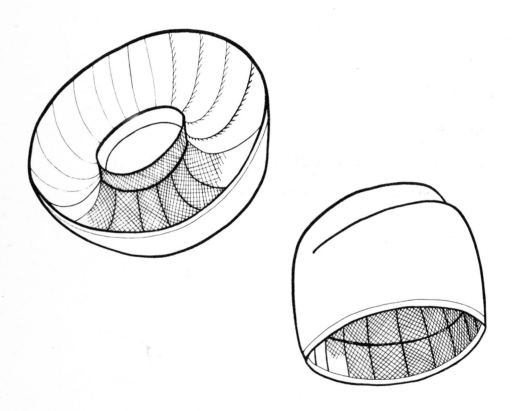

Figure 39 (left)   *Tabbed inside of breton shaped brim*
Figure 40 (right)   *Tabbed and wired inside of shaped crown*

Suppliers

Blockmakers
A H Cooper and Co Ltd
78 Midland Road
Luton, Bedfordshire

General
Fogg and Wakefield
Maddox Street, London W1

R D Franks Limited
Market Place, Oxford Circus, London W1

Rubans de Paris
39a Maddox Street, London W1

These suppliers are normally for trade use although they can be very helpful towards private customers. In addition most large department stores can supply millinery materials and equipment. They are also excellent for trimmings of all kinds.

Local trade and telephone directories are useful for locating suppliers.